To Lee and Robert—
whom I hope will inherit
a more peaceful world

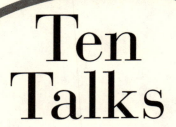

Ten
Talks

Parents Must Have
With Their
Children About

Violence

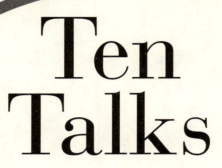

Ten
Talks

Parents Must Have
With Their
Children About

Violence

Dominic Cappello

New York

Library of Congress Cataloging-in-Publication Data

ISBN 0-7868-8549-1

FIRST EDITION

10 9 8 7 6 5 4 3 2 1

Acknowledgments

The Ten Talks Team

The development of *Ten Talks* was a team effort. This book is the result of thousands of conversations with parents, educators, children, and representatives from juvenile justice, police departments, religious organizations, and public health departments from across the country. Packaging their insights into book form involved the invaluable contributions of some very committed colleagues and thoughtful editorial consultants: Bonnie Faddis, Ph.D., a researcher and education specialist in Portland, Oregon; Susan Durón, Ph.D., an education specialist and evaluator in Denver, Colorado; Susan Holmberg, Ph.D., a researcher and media analyst in Seattle, Washington; Susan Burgess, M.S., M.A., an organizational development consultant and therapist in Seattle, Washington; Xenia Becher, M.S.W., C.S.W., in Syracuse, New York, and Paul A. DiDonato, J.D. I am grateful to Pepper Schwartz, Ph.D., an author and sociologist at the University of Washington, who was invaluable in the development of the book's organization. I owe special gratitude to Skylar Fein at Training for Change in

Philadelphia for his candid critique and extensive review of every draft and to Paula Brooks for her reviewing and transcribing of the talks with parents and children.

I am indebted to my national reviewers and advisors: Christine Luong; Susan Coots; April Roseman, M.A., M.P.H.; Elaini Gardiner; Lauri Halderman; Laurie Trotta; Kate Folb; Michael Day; Lisa Frank; Nancy Tartt; Betsy Nagle-McNaughton; Susan Martin; Lisa Perry; Ted Eytan, M.D.; Norma Straw; Mary Jo McHaney; Sharon Eagan; Brad Buckwalter; Aubyn Gwinn; Rita Creighton; Diana Rivera; Suzanne Hidde; Dennis Worsham; Julia Mitchell; Leah Hall; John Henry Kuhlmann; Brooke McDonald; Richard Pargament, and Greg Williamson. I also want to thank our family reviewers: Joe Brooks and his sons Lee and Robert; Norman Vinner and his children Justin and Caitlin; Cynthia Dove and her son Cortez; Kenneth and Patricia Goodling and their daughter Anne; brothers Christopher and Jonathan Pool; Patricia Sorensen and her daughter Kimberly; Grace Richards and her children Jared, Laura, Sarah, and David; Pam Parr and her daughter Betsy; Gabriel Romero and his daughters Gabriela and Anastasia; and Val Dunne, Meagan Baker, and Caitlin Baker.

Special thanks to Jerald Newberry, Paul Sathrum, and Vicki Harrison at the National Education Association Health Information Network for their strong support of the "Can We Talk?" parent-child communication program and their commitment to health promotion for parents, youth, and educators. I also wish to acknowledge Nan Stein, Ed.D., the creator of *Flirting or Hurting, Bullyproof,* and *Gender Violence/Gender Justice,* at the Center for Research on Women, Wellesley College, for her inspiring work in the field of harassment prevention. Thanks to Jerry Painter and Frieda Takamura at the Washington Education Association, Debra Delgado at the Annie E. Casey Foundation, and Lynne Whitt and Kristina Rudiger at the National Center for Health Education. Special thanks to Fred Morris for nurturing *Ten Talks* through its many stages, and to my wise and patient editor at Hyperion, Mary Ellen O'Neill.

Of course, this book would not have been possible without the thousands of parents across the country who attended my workshops and helped me refine the *Ten Talks* approach. Those moms and dads proved that parents are the experts, and with the right resources can nurture family talks about controversial social issues. A big thank-you to the families in Dayton, Georgia; New York, Syracuse, and Jamestown, New York; Seattle, Yakima, Vancouver, and Everett, Washington; Portland, Bend, and Salem, Oregon; San Antonio and Dallas, Texas; Memphis, Tennessee; Kansas City, Missouri; Pine Ridge Indian Reservation, South Dakota; Flint, Michigan; Orlando and Miami, Florida; Asheville, Greenville, Lafayette, and Charlotte, North Carolina; and Virginia Beach and Fairfax, Virginia.

Contents

Contents

Welcome to Ten Talks

How to Use This Book

I always wonder whenever I hear about a man beating or killing someone. What were these men like when they were in fourth grade?—Emily, mother of one, Kansas City, Missouri

My mind is clear and I am not sick.—From a signed statement by Kipland Kinkel, who pleaded guilty to killing four people (including his parents) and wounding twenty-two students in Springfield, Oregon, when he was fifteen years old

Talking about violence gives parents an opportunity to see into their children's lives—to get to know their everyday fears, concerns and hopes.—Pepper Schwartz, Ph.D., University of Washington

Parents are the ones who model the loving, respectful, and responsible behavior they want their sons and daughters to have.
—April Roseman, psychotherapist, Seattle, Washington

A Child's Real World

How violent is your child's world? And, more importantly, how does your child feel about the violence in her life? The answers may surprise you or may even shock you. But getting these answers never has been as important as it is today.

Across the country, parents are sitting down with their children

1

and starting conversations about violence and ways to keep safe. Families are talking about a complex and rapidly changing world—one in which images of violence are pervasive, and where random acts of killing shatter our sense of safety.

Why is raising a child today different from in the past? Families, schools, communities, and the media have changed dramatically in the past few decades. Kids have far more unsupervised time as parents work more and must often raise children in one-parent households. Schools are struggling to meet the needs of diverse student populations, and teachers are being asked to serve as social workers, psychologists, crowd control managers, and life-skills educators. Community life, once centered around small town centers, with influence coming from places of worship and nearby grandparents, is now dispersed throughout suburbs and shopping malls. Broadcast media, which once consisted of a few radio stations and a black-and-white television with four stations that went off the air at midnight, now include network, cable, Internet, and radio programming available twenty-four hours a day, seven days a week. Much of the media's programming, whether packaged as news or entertainment, is spectacularly violent. All of this is taking place in a society where guns have always been available with few restrictions. If you think child rearing today is complex and challenging, you are in good company.

Why Ten Talks?

For the past five years, I have traveled around the country talking with parents about how to open up the lines of communication with their children. As a consultant working for everything from federally funded health programs and national teacher associations to local parent groups, my job is to help communities develop programs that support parent involvement in education. In talking about violence in their children's lives and how to keep them safe, parents are saying that they want to talk with their children about preventing violence, and they need help to do the job right. *Ten Talks* is designed to do exactly that. This book will help you begin a series of family talks that will give your children the skills they need to avoid violent situations and stay safe.

How to Use This Book

Each chapter focuses on a different aspect of violence and is divided into four sections. In the first section, Preparing for the Talk, you will find ways to clarify your values about certain types of violent behavior. You will also explore how you might develop family rules and guidelines on keeping safe. The second section, The Talk, is centered around stories for you and your child to read together, as well as illustrations to help set the scene in your child's mind. These stories illustrate challenging situations that your child might find herself in. Each story is followed by questions for you to ask your child. Your child's answers will give you insight into how she thinks and acts in particular situations. The questions encourage your child to share her views, and may help you articulate your personal values and the importance of following family rules and guidelines. The third section, After the Talk, gives you an opportunity to reflect on your child's responses and to identify any potential problems.

The fourth section contains a sample talk with transcripts of actual talks between a parent and a child. Some talks are very animated and show what can happen when a child is fully engaged.

Others illustrate what happens when a child starts squirming from the moment the parent initiates the conversation. However, even conversations with reluctant children show that they learn something about the topic, and the parents learn more about the child. Each of the ten talks may range from five minutes to an unhurried hour. Even a five-minute talk should be considered successful.

Every Talk Is a Success

When you are discussing heavy subjects with a child, you will not always get full and complete comprehension, or even cooperation. You may not get any reassurance—you may not get any feedback at all. But even when you don't think you've made an impact, take heart; you've expressed concern in these moments between you and your child. There is no wasted effort. And remember that the next time around, your child may surprise you with an astonishingly mature answer. It's happened time and again.

One, Two, or Ten Talks

You know your child best. Not every chapter may pertain to your child's life and family situation, so pick and choose the chapters that make the most sense to you. Also, each chapter contains more than one story—you do not need to read each one with your child for the talk to be effective. You may wish to change the sequence of the talks depending on your interests or the interests of your child. There are two chapters, however, that you should not skip: Chapter One: Talking about Violence and Safety, and Chapter Two: Talking about Victims, Victimizers, and Observers. Each chapter will help you establish a shared vocabulary with your child.

What Can You Expect from Ten Talks*?*

Stick with the ten conversations and you may

- increase the amount of time you spend in meaningful discussions with your child.
- increase your understanding of your child's views about violence.
- feel more confident that your child can keep herself safe.
- be able to describe your family rules about violence and safety.

Do these objectives seem daunting? Don't worry, there won't be a test! *Ten Talks* is about having meaningful conversation with your child, rather than making sure your child comes up with the right answer. You may be thinking, "Can I really do this?" Yes, you can. Thousands of parents in cities across the country already are. Remember that you are an expert when it comes to your child, but even experts need resources and tools to do their jobs well.

The Role of School

When you start to talk with your child about violence, be prepared to hear, "I've already learned this in school." Remember, even if your child's teachers are providing lessons on violence prevention, these lessons are *not* a substitute for communicating your values and house rules on a variety of topics. This means, for better or worse, that the ultimate responsibility for violence prevention education rests with the parents—in other words, you.

Yes, There Is Help

If you get nervous or stressed at the thought of having these talks with your child, consider asking for some help from another adult—a grandparent, aunt, uncle, step-parent, trusted friend, or someone from your religious community. For example, a single mom might want to have a male friend or relative talk with her son about some of these issues. She might turn to the child's grandfather, uncle, or other trusted adult. If you ask another adult to talk with your child, make sure her or his values are compatible with yours. When a parent enlists the help of another adult, it is not an invitation to hand off the responsibility of educating the child. Ultimately, parents have to communicate to their child the house rules. Samples of house rules are illustrated throughout each chapter. If you have any problems enforcing your house rules, again, seek help. Your effort is sure to be rewarded.

Talking with the Noncommunicative Child

When you sit down to have your first talk, your child may make a face that suggests gagging on a foul-tasting substance, followed by rolling eyes and a quick exit. Don't worry, you're not alone in trying to engage a less-than-enthusiastic child. Here are five common ways your child may try to derail the discussion.

Child's rejection #1: "I've already learned this in school."
Child's rejection #2: "I'll talk about this, but I don't want to talk about this with you."
Child's rejection #3: "I'm too busy."
Child's rejection #4: "I'm not gonna do it."
Child's rejection #5: "It's none of your business."

Here are some ways other parents have steered their conversations back on track.

I might have felt the same thing if my mom had asked me to have this talk, but would you first try one talk with me for five minutes and see how it goes?—Roma, mother of two, Costa Mesa, California

Your health and safety are my business. And one way to make sure you stay safe is to tell you my values and learn yours.
—Ed, father of one, San Francisco, California

This is part of my homework as a parent. I help you with your homework, so can you help me with mine?
—Connie, mother of four, Chicago, Illinois

If all else fails, each talk contains a section called The Bare Minimum, for a quick review of terms and family rules. You also may find that talking with your child one on one, rather than with other people present, will give you the best results. And remember that some places are better than others to initiate a talk. Some parents have had their best luck in—of all places—the car. One mom in Seattle said that talking while driving was perfect for her son: He didn't have to maintain eye contact with her, and he couldn't escape!

Family Rules: Your Duty as a Parent

We live in a complicated and potentially dangerous society where we no longer can indulge our children's reluctance to talk about violence. At the very least, you need to come up with some family rules about violence and safety, communicate them to your child, and review them to make sure your child understands them.

We may have two values in this house—yours and mine—but there is only one set of family rules. I want to repeat the family rules to make sure we both understand them.
—Lonnie, mother of two, Kansas City, Missouri

I always assumed that my kids knew the rules about hitting and everything else. But when I asked them what our family rules were, they drew blank stares. I realized my wife and I needed to sit down with them and make the rules very clear.
—Andrew, father of three, Fairfax, Virginia

When Is a Child Old Enough for Ten Talks?

Ten Talks may be used with children from kindergarten to twelfth grade. Younger children can benefit from talks on violence too, as long as you use words that are simple and easy to understand. Many of the aspects of violence illustrated in *Ten Talks* already will be familiar to them through TV or life at school. The main ingredient of the *Ten Talks* process—storytelling—is an activity young children are familiar with. Children in grades four through eight might be the most receptive to these talks. They are old enough to understand the concepts of safety and violence prevention, yet young enough to seek guidance from parents. High school students may see this book as something for "kids," but the family rules outlined in each chapter are relevant to any child living under your roof. If your child watches TV, uses the Internet, or goes to school, then the ten topics in this book need to be discussed. You know best how you can frame the talks in a way that your child will understand.

You will find that your child's reaction to the talks will differ as she moves from elementary school to middle school to high school. Just as a good schoolteacher does, you can revisit the topics in this book yearly to reinforce the lessons learned, review the family rules, and make adjustments if needed.

About Quotes and Pronouns

Many of the quotes from parents and youths come from the workshops on parent-child communication I conducted across the country. The names have been changed to protect the privacy of the workshop attendees. Also, in the interest of succinctness, *Ten Talks* alternates pronouns throughout the text. Thus, in one paragraph we may refer to your child as "she" and in the next as "he."

Special Note

Ten Talks has been developed to help parents and children talk about violence and how to prevent it. *Ten Talks* is not intended to replace professional evaluation and treatment by a licensed mental health professional if needed. For any concerns about a family member's violent behavior or any other significant emotional problems, please contact a licensed child psychologist, psychiatrist, physician, or social worker.

1

What Is Violence?

Talking about Violence and Safety

I tell parents to start early and talk with their children about violence—hearing threats or spotting any guns at school. I started talking with my son when he was in second grade.
—Daryl L. Duchess, police chief, Frewsburg, New York

It may seem obvious, but children need to be told that anger is a normal and healthy emotion. The goal is for children and adults to learn how to express anger nonviolently.
—Susan Burgess, therapist, Seattle, Washington

We were saying a prayer before dinner and my third grade son said, "I pray I don't get beat up at school."
—Pam, mother of two, Gaithersburg, Maryland

How in the world do you begin to talk with a child about a topic as huge and complex as violence? Quite literally, one talk at a time. Our first talk outlines how you and your child define violence.

What do you consider a violent act? Would your child agree with you? A cartoon character hits another over the head with a baseball bat. Is that violence? If so, then by the time most children have started school they have viewed thousands of incidents of violence on TV. Kids on the playground shoot each other with toy guns. Is this violence? As early as first grade, students encounter the school bully and learn very quickly about the power of size and force. Are they encountering violence?

You may be surprised by your child's answers to these questions. What some parents call violence their children might call their "favorite TV show," "a fun electronic game," "a great movie," or "just the way guys are."

The talk in this chapter will provide you with opportunities to discuss how your child defines violence and how safe your child feels. *Ten Talks* makes no assumptions about your child's experience with violence. For some children, life always has been peaceful, barring a few TV shows their parents would prefer they didn't watch. For others, violence and intimidation may be a regular occurrence.

Even though the talk is about violence, this conversation between you and your child is not about frightening or intimidating her to the point that she doesn't want to leave her bedroom. Quite the opposite is true. This talk is about empowering your child by giving her skills, primarily communication and critical-thinking skills. These skills can provide her with the tools she needs to navigate through her daily life.

Preparing for the Talk

This talk opens the door for ongoing conversations that will deepen your child's understanding of violence and safety.

In this talk you will let your child know that

- it's okay to talk about these kinds of topics.
- he can depend on you for support when facing problems about violence.

- you have expectations about her behavior as it relates to violence and safety.
- there are family rules about violence, safety, and how people are to be treated.

What You Can Expect from This Talk

After the talk your child will

- be able to identify violent behavior.
- understand that there are many forms of violence.
- understand your family rules about violence and safety.

How Do You Define Violence?

Your child learns about violence from you. How you define violence has an impact on your child's perspectives. Think about the following behaviors. Do they involve violence, a threat of violence, nonviolence, or are you not sure?

- A student at school yells something cruel about another student's family.
- A student grabs at another boy's shirt, ripping it.
- A child pushes another child.
- A bigger student tells a child to hand over his lunch money.
- A student tells another child that he has a gun the child can use.
- A guy on the basketball court pushes another guy while playing basketball.
- Someone paints "You all will die" on your child's school wall.
- An older boy yells at his girlfriend, "I don't want you talking to other guys."

- On the bus, a child throws a crumpled ball of paper in another's face.

Do you think the behaviors listed above involve violence or the threat of violence? You may be surprised to hear that some parents would say yes, every item on the list involves at least a threat of violence. Others would disagree and describe these behaviors as normal for young people. There are no right or wrong answers here. The goal of this survey is to give you a chance to reflect on how *you* define violence. Do you think you and your child differ in your views on what constitutes violent behavior? As you read through this chapter, there will be opportunities to discuss your definition of violence, along with your personal values, with your child.

Your Home, Your Rules

Alex and his little brother Jesse are folding clothes in the basement when Alex throws the laundry basket at Jesse's head. Jesse's eye is cut and he comes upstairs crying. When his mother goes downstairs to confront Alex, he says, "We were just playing." Alex's mom responded this way: "In our house, we do not throw things at each other. I don't care if it's playing or not. You hurt your brother and you didn't even come upstairs to see if he was all right. You are grounded for the weekend."

Your response to the situation above might be different. Some parents might excuse such roughhousing. Others might want the brother to apologize but may not want to punish him. The point is that the mom has articulated a family rule about hitting others. She has also imposed consequences for breaking family rules.

Some families have a lot of rules in their homes. Other families don't. *Ten Talks* refers to family rules throughout. Family rules are also known as "guidelines" or "expectations for your behavior."

If you were to ask your child, "What are the family rules about violence in our home?" what would she say? A goal of *Ten Talks* is to help you identify and set the rules that you feel comfortable with and to make sure that your child knows what they are.

When I grew up my mom never said anything about rules except, "Don't hit your sister." But I just figured hitting was what everybody did when parents or teachers weren't looking.
—Lydia, mother of two, Rockville, Maryland

My mom and dad never hit us. I was shocked to see that my friends' parents would smack them. But my friends would say that it was no big deal.—Vicki, mother of three, Montgomery Village, Maryland

My mom and dad were very thoughtful people and great parents. They were also survivalists who had a lot of guns and other weapons. But I never thought of my parents as violent at all. They just said we had to be prepared.—Bob, father of one, Jamestown, New York

Influence of the Media

The media often broadcasts images of violence as entertainment. These images are not designed to offer insights into the complex issues surrounding violent behavior. That's your job.

Popular media, including TV, films, music, and videos, play a big role in portraying violence. Because the media rarely examine their own treatment of violence, it leaves the definition of violence, and the separation of reality and fantasy, to parents. While the impact of violent TV programming on young people is debated in many circles, two characteristics of the American popular media are clear: first, that violence is portrayed as an integral part of life, and second, that violence is often portrayed as heroic. Alternatives to violence using conflict resolution are almost minimal at best. In Chapter Four, violence in the media is explored in greater detail.

Pressure from Peers

I've traveled around the country helping parents communicate with their children about violence. I always ask parents to think back to their own childhoods and what motivated them. Nearly everyone has the same answer: peer pressure. Parents say that pressure from peers was the single largest factor influencing their decisions, from how they treated people to experimenting with drugs and sex.

You may remember how important it was as a child to be accepted by your peers. This kind of pressure probably increased as you moved from elementary to middle to high school. The talk you will have with your child will help foster communication about the relationship between peer pressure and getting into and out of potentially violent situations.

Peer pressure was my biggest downfall from age twelve on up. I've just managed to get it under control, now that I'm a mother!
—Mary, mother of one, New York City

Giving Your Child the Big Picture

How large a role does violence play in your child's life? It depends on many factors. Consider the following statistics:

Number of violent crimes committed against juveniles in 1997: 600,000

(Source: Federal Interagency Forum on Child and Family Statistics)

Number of school-shooting deaths in 1997–98: 40
(Source: National School Safety Center, Pepperdine University)

What do these numbers mean to your family's life and well-being? As you can see, children are often the victims of violent crime. The majority of those incidents are not occurring at school, as the news might suggest, but at home and in the neighborhood. The statistics show that no matter who you are, what your income is, or where you live, violent behavior is a part of life. Some of it can't be prevented, but much of it can.

The good news is that you have considerable control over the development of your child's attitudes about violence and safety. These attitudes start developing in the home. You are the most important influence on your child. You are the role model for expressing anger, communicating frustrations, and finding alternatives to violence.

My dad would just blow up and yell when he was mad. Waiting for him to blow was worse than the actual yelling. I've worked on that myself and made a conscious decision not to display my anger the way my dad did.—Don, father of three, Fredonia, New York

Points of View

In general, violent behavior affects the lives of males and females differently. Males tend to be more violent than females. Males instigate the majority of violence in the U.S., and it's usually against other males. Is it nature or nurture that's making men this way—or a combination of both? Two therapists sum up a variety of theories:

Some people say the culprit is testosterone—that male violence is a product of natural selection. Maybe it's a holdover from primitive territorial drives. Nowadays there's a broad consensus among psychoanalysts that some part of violent behavior is biologically based, but that it's far from inevitable. Violence may be part of nature, but it's the parents' job to create a peaceful individual who can control violent impulses.—Susan Burgess, therapist, Seattle, Washington

Is it nature or nurture? From what I've observed in therapy, aside from brain damage and chemical imbalance, it's typically nurture. Children are survival-oriented and they model their surrounding behavior to learn the lessons of survival. They model everything. Violent children are angry children—and I believe that the physical, emotional and sexual abuse of children is what causes much of their anger and violence. Angry, acting-out parents will produce angry, acting-out children. Abusive parents will produce angry children. Anger is a normal response to the abnormal experience of abuse.
—April Roseman, psychotherapist, Seattle, Washington

Author Richard Rhodes has his own theory of how people turn violent. In his book *Why They Kill: Discoveries of a Maverick Criminologist*, the Pulitzer Prize-winning author outlines a process that he says all violent people go through. In the first stage, a child is forced to submit to violence, usually by an authority figure. In the second stage, the child comes to believe that violence is necessary to survive from day to day. Next, the young person tries out violence, and it succeeds; people fear and respect him. As the child grows, he decides more and more that violence works—he likes the feeling of power and control. And in the meantime, the voices of his early "violence coaches" continue to echo in his head, reinforcing the message that violence is his prime survival tool. Rhodes's model is unique because it doesn't depend on genes, social class, race, or mental illness to explain violence.

If we all believed that biology is destiny, we would have to shut this book and just endure the rage of males. Fortunately, as most family counselors point out, there may be social and cultural factors that predispose a male to violence, and if we address these factors we may be able to raise less violent sons. We need to challenge the male belief that boys and men are entitled to be violent, act tough, and solve problems with physical strength. We need to give males and females the communication skills to express their angry feelings and frustrations.

The question of whether bad behavior is preprogrammed genetically is one of the central controversies in child development. An informed starting point is to remember that child development requires the interplay of biology and society, the characteristics children bring with them into the world and the way the world treats them, nature and nurture.—James Garbarino, Ph.D., in *Lost Boys: Why Our Sons Turn Violent and How We Can Help Them*

We have a lot to do when it comes to raising our sons and daughters. They all have the potential to become violent. Boys and girls can present different challenges to parents. We need to raise sons to be communicative and caring and to find alternatives to violence. We need to raise daughters to be strong, assertive, and to reject the role of victim.
—Susan Durón, Ph.D., Denver, Colorado

It's about testosterone. I've told both my daughters that guys are just more explosive. Not all guys, but a lot of them. They tell me from what they see in sixth and ninth grade that I'm right. But they also tell me that some guys seem to be okay.
—Betty, mother of two, Portland, Oregon

Different Families: Different Values

Your child is presented with many values about violence. You have your values and rules. But your child's friends, teachers, or coaches may have different ones. The following scenarios illustrate how your child may receive different messages weekly.

Your child is playing at a neighbor's home with a group of boys. One boy grabs your son's electronic game right out of his hands and pushes him away, calling him a name.

The friend's mom sees this altercation. She thinks this is acceptable, and just "kids being kids." How would you react?

■

In gym class, a sixth grader throws a basketball at your son's back, knocking him to the ground, and then laughs.

The coach sees this altercation and thinks this is normal roughhousing. He feels it's up to the students to work out their own problems. How would you want to see this situation addressed?

■

A boy and your daughter are talking on the sidewalk in front of your home. Her new boyfriend comes up, grabs her arm, and pulls her away, saying, "I don't want you talking to other guys." Your daughter goes along with her boyfriend, thinking that his act of possessiveness is flattering.

You view this altercation. Would you want your daughter to say something to the boyfriend about his behavior? Would you tell her that his behavior is not healthy?

The neighbor's mom, the coach, and the boyfriend all have their own values about violence. In real life, your child faces situations similar to these all the time. Other people are communicating their values to your child in subtle or not-so-subtle ways. Your values need to be communicated in a way that's equally loud and clear.

Last-minute Checkups before the Talk

This is a good time to think about your childhood experiences with violence.

- Did a parent ever tell you not to hit others?
- Were you allowed to watch violent programs on TV?
- Did you ever tell your parents about violent behavior at school? What did they say?
- Did your family ever discuss weapons, and their safe and legal use?
- Did they ever talk to you about inappropriate touching and what you could do in response to it?

How do you think your childhood experiences have affected the way you raise your child?

- Have you told your child not to hit others?
- Have you told her to expect some violent behavior at school? Is she supposed to avoid aggressive kids?
- Do you have rules on what kind of violent programming your child can watch?
- Have you talked about weapons and their safe and legal use?
- Has your family discussed inappropriate touching and how people can respond to it?

Do you have any stories that you could share with your child? For example:

- A story about a neighbor or schoolmate who threatened you
- An experience confronting a bully
- A time when an adult explained the difference between feeling angry and being violent
- A story about how you avoided a violent situation

Keep these stories in mind as you talk with your child. She needs to hear that you have faced these situations and survived.

What Are Your Family Rules?

Do you have family rules about hitting, pushing, and unwanted touching? If not, this is a good time to think about them. The talk outlined in this chapter highlights the following situations:

- A big kid threatens a smaller child and demands his lunch money.
- A brother threatens to hit his smaller sister for breaking his CD player.
- A boy grabs his girlfriend's arm and yanks her along, trying to control her behavior.
- A man and woman fight at the bus stop.

Discussing these situations will give you an opportunity to discuss your family rules. What would you want your child to do in each situation? What are your expectations? Before the talk, think about what rules you want to communicate to your child. At the end of the talk, you will have the chance to review the rules with your child.

The Talk

All right—you are almost ready to have the talk about defining violence with your child. To fully understand the *Ten Talks* process, make sure to read the entire chapter before starting the talk. You may find the sample talks at the end of this chapter particularly helpful.

Introduce the Talk

Find a time for an uninterrupted ten minutes or so. With this book in hand, tell your child: "I'm reading this book about violence. I need to talk to you for five or ten minutes."

Some younger children may be happy to talk with you, but others will be uninterested. Many children assume that they actually know more about real life than you do. A common response is, "I already know all this."

If your child doesn't want to talk, be patient. Many parents report that their children don't get enthusiastic until the third or fourth talk. And remember, you can use the following statement as many times as necessary: "It's part of my job as a parent to have this talk, to listen to you, and answer your questions. It's part of your job as my child to listen and ask me questions."

Remember that children don't want to be talked down to or to be treated like babies. At the first sign of patronizing speech, they shut down. Remember how you liked to be spoken to when you were young.

Next, you could say, "I've got a few questions to discuss. First, can you give me some examples of violence?"

Your child may offer some examples. If so, proceed with the next section.

If he doesn't offer examples of violence, say something like, "There are many different kinds of violence. Some of it we see as entertainment. Some of it is illegal and deadly. Examples of violence might include murder or armed robbery. There is also unwanted touching, pushing, name-calling, threats of violence, intimidation, and sexual words hurled at you. Violence also can be seen on TV, in films, and in sports."

Review These Words

Please review the terms in this section. Discussing all the terms with your child is optional. You know what's appropriate for your child's age and maturity level. Keep in mind that more than likely, even the youngest children have heard these words on TV.

abuse: to misuse something or someone
assault: to attack something or someone
family rules: the guidelines each family has in place to describe acceptable and unacceptable behavior
intimidation: to make afraid, as with threats
safety: to feel protected
threats: to challenge someone's sense of safety
violence: showing or acting with wild force or feeling. Acts of violence may range from mild pushing and shoving to slapping, slugging, and causing life-threatening bodily harm.

Why Is Talking about Violence Important?

Ask your child whether she thinks talking about violence is important. Here are some reasons you might want to offer:

- Talking about violence helps us identify violent behavior.
- Talking about violence helps us learn how to deal with violence.
- Talking about violence helps us learn how to treat others.

- Talking about violence helps us clarify our family rules on staying safe.

The Stories

In the next part of the talk, you'll be reading short stories to your child and discussing them together. You don't have to read all of the stories. Pick the ones that you think are appropriate for your child. The stories are very simple. Feel free to embellish them, adding details that you think might make the story more believable to your child. For example, some parents change the gender of the characters to make the story mirror their own families.

Some children will express their concerns in a straightforward way. Others may say, "Well, I know this kid at school who has some problems," when they're really talking about themselves. Remember that you may have to read between the lines to get to your child's true feelings and concerns.

The Story about Lunch Money

Read this story to your child. This story provides an opportunity to discuss intimidation.

"It's lunchtime at school. Lots of students are walking around the cafeteria. A big student walks up to a smaller student. He tells the smaller boy to give him his lunch money."

The discussion questions that follow will allow you to find out how she feels about intimidation and threats of violence.

Ask these questions of your child:

- What does the big student say?
- What does the smaller student say?
- What is the big student thinking?
- What is the smaller student thinking?

Now that your child has completed this scenario, ask the following questions:

- What can happen to the smaller student if he doesn't hand over the money?
- What can happen to the smaller student if he does hand over the money?
- Is this an example of a threat of violence? Why?
- Is this an example of violence? Why?
- How often does this type of thing really happen?
- Have you ever seen or been in a situation like this? If so, how did you feel? What did you do?
- What would be the best thing to do if you were being threatened in a situation like this?

Clarify Your Family's Values

Discuss these questions with your child as a way of sharing your values about behavior. A number of potential responses from children are included to help you formulate your own responses.

Ask your child: "When a person is threatened with violence, what can he do?"

Child response #1: Nothing.
Parent: Nothing? Maybe it depends on the situation. If it involves fighting one on one, what can you do?
Child: Depends on how big the guy is.
Parent: If he is bigger than you?
Child: Run or fight or talk your way out of it.
Parent: If you run away, what might happen later? How can you talk your way out of this situation?

Child response #2: Fight back.
Parent: If you don't fight back what can you do?

Child response #3: Tell somebody.
Parent: Who can you tell? What can happen to you if you do that?

Child response #4: Get my friends to get the guy later.
Parent: Is getting even going to solve the problem?
Child: Yes.
Parent: Let's review some family rules about being threatened, fighting back, and revenge.

The Story about Brothers and Sisters

This story gives you an opportunity to discuss how siblings interact, set personal boundaries, and express anger.

"A girl is playing and drops and breaks her older brother's CD player. The brother is angry and raises his hand as if he is going to hit her."

Ask these questions of your child:

- What is the brother saying?
- What is the sister saying?
- What is the brother thinking?
- What is the sister thinking?

Now that your child has completed this scenario, ask the following questions:

- Is this an example of the threat of violence?
- Is this an example of violence?
- Is breaking the CD player an act of violence?
- What can the brother do to express his anger that doesn't involve hitting?
- What would the kids' parents say about this situation?
- Have you seen or been in a situation like this? If so, how did you feel? What did you do?
- What would be the best thing to do if you were being threatened in a situation like this?

Clarify Your Family's Values

Discuss these questions with your child as a way of sharing your values about behavior.

Ask your child: "What can someone do, aside from hitting, when a person makes him angry?"

Child response #1: That's the only way to make a point sometimes.
Parent: Hitting is only one option. What are others?

Child response #2: Yell.
Parent: Yelling is better than hitting. Talking is better than yelling. When a person calms down people usually can talk more
   reasonably.

Child response #3: I don't know.
Parent: Let's talk about our family rules on this topic of expressing anger.

Stories for Older Children

The following stories deal with controlling behavior and observing adults being violent. While some younger children may not be
able to relate to them, you may find that to your child, these stories make perfect sense.

The Story about Controlling

This story provides an opportunity to
discuss controlling behavior.

"A girl is at a store with her boyfriend. The boy tells the girl he wants to
leave the store and the girl says she wants

to stay. The boy grabs the girl by the arm and starts pulling her toward the door. He is serious about leaving the store now."

Ask these questions of your child:

- What is the girl thinking?
- What is the boy thinking?
- What is the girl saying?
- What is the boy saying?

Now that your child has completed this scenario, ask the following questions:

- How is this an example of the threat of violence?
- How is this an example of violence?
- What should the girl do?
- How is the girl feeling?
- Why would the boy do something like that?
- What happens if the girl tells the boy to stop and he doesn't?
- Does the boy have the right to make his girlfriend do what he wants? Why?
- How would the situation be different if the roles were reversed?
- Have you ever seen or been in a situation like this? If so, how did you feel? What did you do?
- What would be the best thing to do if you were being pulled in a situation like this?

Clarify Your Family's Values

Discuss these questions with your child as a way of sharing your values about behavior.

Ask your child: "What can someone do when a boyfriend or girlfriend tries to control his or her behavior?"

Child response #1: What do you mean?
Parent: If a boy tries to get his girlfriend to do everything he wants and gets angry with her if she disagrees with him, that means he is being controlling.

Child response #2: She can tell him to stop it.
Parent: Yes. She can explain that she does not appreciate his controlling behavior. How would a boyfriend or girlfriend react to being told that?

Child response #3: If she wants to keep him she may have to go along with him.
Parent: Is that a good thing for her to do? Let's talk about what makes a healthy relationship, how both people in a relationship can compromise, and how good friendships are balanced.

The Story about the People at the Bus Stop

This story is an opportunity to discuss expressing anger and threatening behavior.

"A little boy is waiting for a bus. Up walks a teenage couple holding hands. As they all wait for the bus, the couple start to argue. The man grabs the woman by the shoulders. The man begins to shake the woman harshly as he yells. The woman starts crying. It looks like the man is getting angrier."

Ask these questions of your child:

- What is the woman thinking?
- What is the man thinking?
- What is the little boy thinking?

Now that your child has completed this scenario, ask the following questions:

- How is this an example of the threat of violence?
- How is this an example of violence?
- What should the woman do?
- How is the woman feeling?
- Why would the man do something like that?
- What happens if the woman tells the man to stop and he doesn't?
- Where can people get help if they are in an abusive relationship?
- Have you ever seen or been in a situation like this? If so, how did you feel? What did you do?
- What would be the best thing to do if you were observing a situation like this?

Clarify Your Family's Values

Discuss these questions with your child as a way of sharing your values about behavior.

Ask your child: "When a person tries to control the behavior of another person, can this kind of attitude and behavior lead to threats of violence?"

Child response #1: I don't know.
Parent: Controlling behavior can lead to violent behavior. Can you see how that can happen?

Child response #2: Maybe.
Parent: The need to control others is not always healthy. What might happen to people who get into relationships where one does the controlling and the other accepts being controlled?

Child response #3: How do you know what's healthy?
Parent: Let's talk about our family rules on this topic of how we treat friends. We can also talk about healthy, respectful relationships and how people in those relationships don't try to control each other.

The Bare Minimum: A Quick Quiz for Kids
Ask your child the following questions to assess her knowledge of violence.

1. What is violence?
   Sample answers: hitting, threats, intimidation, name-calling, shoving, killing, hurting a pet, or abuse of any kind

2. Can you give me one example of how a person might threaten another with violence?
   Sample answers:

- A guy tells another kid to hand over his lunch money.
- A brother threatens to "kill" his sister for breaking his stuff.
- A bully makes another kid do everything the bully wants.
- A girl threatens to spread rumors about another girl who doesn't lend her a dress she wants to wear.
- A neighbor says she will kick your dog when she sees it.

Talk about Your Family Rules

These must be *your* rules. Give careful thought and be prepared for your child to ask about the reasons behind the rules. You may find it helpful to talk with relatives or friends about developing your family rules. Sample answers from parents across the country follow.

Ask your child the following questions:

1. What is our family rule about hitting others?
Sample answers:
- We never hit anyone.
- We don't threaten people with violence of any kind.
- We only use force in self-defense or to get away from a violent situation.

2. What is one family rule about reporting any threats of violence?
Sample answers:
- When you feel threatened in any way by anyone, I want to hear about it.
- When you feel unsafe in any way, I want you to tell me about it.
- If for some reason you feel you can't tell me about threats you receive, then I want you to tell other adults that we have agreed

upon. (The child is given the names and phone numbers of these trusted friends or family members.)

Rewarding Your Child

Some parents don't feel they have to reward their child for having a talk—they think it's just a normal part of being a family. Other parents want to offer the child a special treat as a thank-you for their open and honest communication. Rewards vary from a hug to a trip to the mall to help with homework—one mom jokingly refers to the reward as her barter system!

After the Talk

A Moment to Reflect

Take a moment to reflect on the talk you just had with your child. How do you feel about it?

- What surprised you about your child's perceptions of violent behavior?
- How do you feel about your ability to talk with your child about violence?
- How much of the time were you listening to your child?
- How do you think your child felt about the talk?
- What will you do differently in the next talk?

After the talk with their child, many parents report a variety of feelings—accomplishment at sustaining a five-minute talk of substance, frustration at not being able to get more information from their child, even a sense of fear that their children may be involved in situations they can't handle.

Warning Signs

The talks also may reveal potential problems that your child is facing, whether as the victim or the victimizer. Was your child reluctant to talk about any situations? Did he avoid eye contact or get angry? Did his responses to your questions seem like normal behavior? Or did you get the feeling that something may be wrong?

There may be cause for concern if you hear from the school or from other parents or child-care providers that your child

- is touching other children inappropriately.
- expresses extreme hatred toward others.
- is afraid of another child.
- is submissive to another child.
- feels bossed around by a boyfriend or girlfriend.
- gets sick a lot and wants to skip school or a particular class, like gym.

In any of these situations, you need to find out what is happening by talking with your child. If, after your discussion, you feel your child needs more help than you alone can offer, visit the school counselor or social worker for resources available in your community.

Finding Help

If needed, support and help for your child is available. Most schoolteachers and principals, religious leaders, mental health center staff, and juvenile justice center staff can refer parents to professionals with expertise in working with young people. Often a short-term intervention can do a world of good. If you have a good relationship with your child's grandparents or other extended family members, tell them what's going on with your child and seek out the kind of support you and your child need.

Success Stories

You have made it through talk number one. It's a good beginning. Many parents say that getting their kids to have the first talk was like pulling teeth. And some of the things they found out weren't pretty. In the course of the talks, some children told stories of school bullies, violent neighbors, and even problems between siblings. Other children shared great news—about how they can spot and steer clear of bullies, or about how they managed to end arguments with siblings without their hitting each other. One mom in Memphis, Tennessee, was surprised to hear that her son had given a lot of thought to the local bullies; he'd even figured out how to avoid them at the bus stop by showing up there seconds, rather than minutes, before the bus arrived.

But no matter what you've heard from your child, you've started an important process, and one with a powerful ripple effect. You're now raising a child whose family discusses violence, and whose parents don't shy away from discussing vital issues like safety and personal boundaries. You've become the rare family that addresses these topics openly and honestly. You're the rare parent who's taken the time to listen attentively and get a clearer picture of your child's real world.

Remember, this is only your first talk. Future talks can only become easier. You're planting a seed that may not bear fruit until you've got a few more talks behind you.

Sample Talks

Between Parents and Children

If you are wondering how a talk based on this chapter might really sound, take a look at the following excerpts from real family talks.

Discussing the Story about Lunch Money

Participants: a mother and her fourth-grade son.

Mom: Here is the situation. A big student tells a smaller student to give him his lunch money. When this happens, what is the smaller student thinking?

Child: I don't know. I don't know what kind of person he is. Is he a coward or what?

Mom: What kind of kid do you want the smaller student to be?

Child: Not a coward. So he says, "Go away."

Mom: What is the big student thinking when he is doing this?

Child: That he wants the smaller student's lunch money, and since he is bigger he can have it.

Mom: What does the smaller student say to the bigger student?

Child: "No, go away."

Mom: What does the bigger student say to the smaller student?

Child: "No. Give me your lunch money."

Mom: What can happen to the smaller student if he doesn't hand over the money?

Child: He will get beat up.

Mom: What can happen to the smaller student if he does hand over the money?

Child: He won't get beat up and he'll keep getting picked on.

Mom: Is this an example of a threat of violence?

Child: Yes, if the bully says, "Or else."

Mom: Is this an example of violence?

Child: If he gets beat up, yes.

Mom: How often does this really happen?

Child: Maybe once or twice. Since I'm usually the big kid I really don't know.

Mom: Have you ever seen or been in a situation like this?

Child: No. Nobody bothers me, 'cause I'm bigger.

Mom: Have you seen this happen to anyone else?

Child: No. The principal won't let it happen.

Lessons Learned from This Sample Talk

This parent has some opportunities to probe more deeply into school life. For example, what might happen if the principal wasn't around? How does the child handle himself when he's around older children and isn't the "big kid" in the situation? The parent might also ask the child to explain what he means by "coward" and what his attitudes are about being one.

Discussing the Story about Brothers and Sisters

Participants: a mother and her eighth-grade son.

Mom: A girl is playing and drops and breaks her brother's CD player. The brother is angry and raises his hand as if he is going to hit her. What is the brother thinking?

Child: He's really mad.

Mom: What is the girl thinking?

Child: "Uh-oh!"

Mom: What is the brother saying?

Child: "What were you thinking! Why did you do that? What's the 'scuse?"

Mom: What is the sister saying?

Child: "I didn't mean to. It was an accident."

Mom: Is this an example of the threat of violence?

Child: Yes.

Mom: Is this an example of violence?

Child: No.

Mom: Why?

Child: He didn't do anything yet.

Mom: What could the brother do to express his anger that doesn't involve hitting?

Child: Tell their mom or dad.

Mom: What would the kids' parents say about this situation?

Child: I'm not sure.

Mom: Have you seen or been in a situation like this? If so, how did you feel? What did you do?

Child: Nope. And I don't hit girls.

Lessons Learned from This Sample Talk

In this situation the mother noted that her son has no sisters but he does have a younger brother, whom he has hit on many occasions. The parent has the opportunity to discuss why the child feels he can hit smaller boys but not girls, and whether breaking the CD player might also be an act of violence. Further talks may get the son to talk about his intimidation of his brother.

Discussing the Story about Controlling

Participants: a mom and her fourth-grade daughter.

Mom: This is a story about a boy and his girlfriend who have gone to a store together. The boy wants to leave but the girl doesn't. The boy grabs the girl by the arm and starts pulling her toward the door. What is the girl thinking?

Child: She doesn't know what her friend wants to do.

Mom: What is the boy thinking?

Child: "Oh, come on. I just want to get out of this place."

Mom: And what is the girl saying?

Child: "I really want to stay."

Mom: What is the boy saying?

Child: "I really want to leave."

Mom: Why is this an example of violence?

Child: It's not.

Mom: You don't think it is?

Child: No. He just pulled someone.

Mom: That could be okay? How is this an example of a threat of violence?

Child: By grabbing their arm and threatening that they are going to do something.

Mom: Very good. What should the girl do?

Child: Leave.

Mom: Just go with him?

Child: She doesn't want a fight to get started.

Mom: Why would the boy do something like that? [long pause]

Child: Maybe because he felt like he really wanted to get out of that place?

Mom: What happens if the girl tells the boy to stop and he doesn't?

Child: He might get even madder?

Mom: Have you ever seen or been in a situation like this?

Child: No.

Lessons Learned from This Sample Talk

This parent sat through a lot of silent pauses during this talk. The mom said it was not easy for her daughter to grasp the idea of controlling behavior between boyfriends and girlfriends because she can't relate to the idea of dating. In future talks, the mom has the opportunity to discuss controlling behavior among platonic friends and family members. The mom also may wish to talk about what the girl in the story might do if the boyfriend's controlling behavior continues.

Discussing the Story about the People at the Bus Stop

Participants: a mother and her fifth-grade son.

Mom: A little boy is waiting for a bus. Up walks a teenage couple holding hands. As they all wait for the bus, the couple starts to argue. The girl wants to spend time with one of her girlfriends, but the boy wants her to go out with him. The boy grabs his girlfriend by the shoulders. He begins to shake her violently as he yells. The girl starts crying. It looks like the boy might hurt her. What is the girl thinking? She's being shaken now.

Child: Well, "Maybe I'll dump him."

Mom: What is the boy thinking?

Child: "Why won't she go out with me?"

Mom: What is the boy saying?

Child: "Why go out with your girlfriend? Go out with me."

Mom: What is the little boy who's watching thinking?

Child: He might, like, think, "What happened?"

Mom: Okay. Is this an example of violence?

Child: Yes.

Mom: Is this an example of the threat of violence?

Child: No.

Mom: Why?

Child: Because you didn't make the man threatening anyone.

Mom: So because the man is actually shaking his girlfriend, he is actually doing violence to her.

Child: Yeah.

Mom: What could the man do to express his anger that doesn't involve hitting or shaking?

Child: He could say, "I won't like you."

Mom: He could talk to her, you mean?

Child: He could.

Mom: Have you seen or been in a situation like this?

Child: No. I mean I've had arguments with girls but . . .

Mom: You've had an argument with a girl?

Child: Yeah, about what the answer is, like on a test.

Mom: But you didn't start hitting each other?

Child: No. Because then I would be, like, suspended.

Lessons Learned from This Sample Talk

The parent might ask if suspension from school is the only thing that would keep her son from being violent. She might also ask what he thinks might stop adults from hurting each other. The parent might ask: What laws exist to protect people, both young and old, from violence? Are arguments always a form of violence? How can people argue in a way that is healthy? How do you feel when you see people arguing? How did you feel when you had the argument with the girl at school?

2

What's Our Role?

Talking about Victims, Victimizers, and Observers

There are no innocent bystanders when it comes to violence. You are either actively helping prevent violence or you are quietly part of supporting it.—Connie, mother of two, San Antonio, Texas

I'm not gonna say something to the bully or he'll turn on me.
—Mary, fifth grader, Seattle, Washington

Children are observing violence every day. Getting them to take the appropriate action is a challenge. Parents can teach their child to call 911, go to an adult. They can tell their child that it is heroic to call—and often smarter than trying to fix something themselves.
—Pepper Schwartz, Ph.D., University of Washington

It's the typical after-school fight. One guy is more of a bully, pushing and taunting his reluctant opponent, a smaller boy without a support group, who is more a victim of circumstances. The bully has started the fight because he's angry. He doesn't need much of an excuse to lash out. Lots of students are circling the two guys. Your child is one of them. Some of the students are yelling, "Hit him!" or "Kill him!" Other students are just watching. Some actually feel bad for the victim and wish there were something they could do to stop the fight. Others are just glad they are not the one being attacked. Yet, just like drivers slowing down when passing a car wreck, most of the students can't look away. What do you imagine your child would do in this situation?

Take a moment to think about the roles people play when someone becomes violent. There is the victimizer, also known as the bully or attacker. Then there's the victim or target. People also can play the role of observer. This is the person who watches, either passively or actively, an interaction unfold. Occasionally a boy or girl who is observing comes forward to try to stop a violent situation. What's your child's role in violent situations?

If your child is an observer, can you imagine him coming forward to defend the victim? From a child's point of view, opposing the bully can be the equivalent of saying, "Attack *me.*" Would your child risk trading the role of observer for that of victim? Would you want him to?

Preparing for the Talk

This chapter explains the role of victims, victimizers, and observers—roles that children are playing every day. We'll also look at why people become victimizers and how others can deal with their aggressive behaviors. This talk will help you give your child the skills to go safely from observation to intervention when she sees violent behavior. These skills include the importance of finding peer support when intervening in violent situations.

In this talk you will help your child understand that

- everyone plays a role in violent situations, whether victim, victimizer, or observer
- observers are not always "innocent bystanders"
- people can change roles depending on the situation
- there are family rules about observing, initiating, and getting involved in violent situations

What You Can Expect from This Talk

After the talk your child will be able to

- define the terms *victimizer, victim,* and *observer.*
- distinguish between active and passive observers of violence.
- identify how to learn skills in conflict resolution.
- know where to get help when dealing with one's own aggressive feelings.

About Roles

The notion of roles may be familiar to many children. Terms like *victimizer* and *victim* may be understood to them as "bully," "punk" or "wimp." The role of observer might be thought of as "people who watch the fight." An observer also might be one who chooses to intervene in a violent situation, otherwise known as "the big kid who stopped the fight." Perhaps your child has been in one role or even in all of them. The role of observer is the most common and often the most confusing.

How does a person make sure he doesn't become a victimizer?

How do people, either as observers or victims, change the behavior of the victimizer? It starts with changing attitudes. And it involves heroic actions.

In recent years, students who were once passive observers or victims of violent behaviors have begun to take conflict resolution courses, join peer mediation groups, and find advocates for safety in parents and school staff. Troubled, aggressive youths whose violent behaviors were once tolerated and excused as "something to grow out of" are now seen as victimizers, and are receiving appropriate counseling. Those people who had once been victims are finding support and acquiring the skills needed to avoid aggressive people.

What Role Is Your Child Playing?

Every family has its own way of labeling participants in a violent situation. Some victimizers see themselves as victims. Most of these victimizers have come from very troubled homes where violence, in the form of hitting or verbal abuse, is commonplace. They may feel a sense of entitlement which gives them permission to hit or make threats if they feel angry.

Some children who are bullied and intimidated at school or in the neighborhood would not define themselves as victims. They just see themselves as getting through another scary day, often suffering in silence. Some of these children perceive the attention they receive as a victim in positive as well as negative terms.

The label of observer may seem strange to some children. They might think that they are not observers if they happen to watch a fight after school—they are just doing what everyone else does. What roles did you experience growing up—victim, victimizer, or observer?

We need to get children and their parents to come forward and report on the threats they observe. For too long kids and parents thought that it wasn't worth reporting on bullies. Believe me, reporting is being taken very seriously in schools, and everyone needs to be taking part in pointing out the problem makers.
—Scott, father of two and middle school principal, Boise, Idaho

I've talked with my son about standing up for the smaller kids. He's a big guy for his age and can put an end to most fights if he wants to. Even though he's a good kid I don't think he sees being a peacemaker as part of what he should be doing. He says that watching a fight is fun sometimes.
—Carmen, mother of two, Dalton, Georgia

Influence of the Media

Here's one example of how the media shapes our perceptions of the roles people play in violent interactions. Many of us grew up watching the Hollywood westerns in which the bad guy terrorized the town. All the townspeople put their hopes and fate in the hands of a hero (the sheriff or hired gun). It was up to the lone good guy to have the shootout with the lone bad guy while the townspeople looked on passively.

What's wrong with that picture? One hero versus one bad guy, plus one hundred townsfolk as passive observers. This dynamic plays itself out in real life, as one bully intimidates another kid while a large group of students watch and cheer. Is this art imitating life or vice versa?

It's not easy to find films that show how people can work together to solve problems, promote civility, restrain aggressive people, and prevent violent behavior. The message from Hollywood movies is that to save your family and your neighborhood, you need a hero with superhuman skills. It's rare when movies show people working together to solve realistic problems of any kind.

TV is not very helpful when it comes to preparing children for intervening in violent situations. Rarely will students find a hero at the right time and place to put an end to a fight after school. Rather, it is critical to empower children to be aware of their options and to make sound decisions about their own and others' safety.
—Susan Durón, Ph.D., Denver, Colorado

Pressure from Peers to Observe

Your child, like most of us, feels pressure to conform to her peer group. When a fight occurs and students circle to cheer on the winner, how will the pressure to conform to the group—to watch and show approval—impact your child? This is a question of values and strength of character. Ask your child what kinds of fighting, name-calling, and shoving she has observed at school or in the neighborhood. The frequency and quality of the aggressive behaviors witnessed by your child may surprise you. How does she feel when she watches violent behavior? If she wanted to help a student who was the object of a verbal or physical attack, what could she do? Has she ever seen others help in such situations? If your child is receiving instruction on conflict resolution at school, she may have more to say on the subject than would a child who has not been introduced to the concept.

This talk will help you discuss what kinds of unspoken codes of behavior exist in your child's world. If you find out that your child is a passive observer, you need to know what she believes prevents her and her peers from taking an active stand against aggressive behaviors.

The Pressure from Peers to Victimize

Does your child feel pressure to act out aggressively? Is he acting out alone? Is he seeking the acceptance of a group that exhibits violent behavior? There are numerous warning signs to help parents recognize if their child might be prone to violent acts. The National Association of Elementary School Principals' Report to Parents encourages parents to look for these warning signs: a serious change in personality, threatening others, cruelty to animals, an uncontrollable temper, mesmerization by weapons, becoming a loner with no close friends, inability to accept criticism. The report cautions, however, that any of these warning signs alone may be "nothing more than youthful rebellion."

People who are bullies need to be educated. If they're not, they'll grow up to batter their wives and kids.
—Tammy, mother of two, Memphis, Tennessee

I read a lot about zero tolerance for violence or threats in schools. It reminds me of seeing those signs at the airport metal detectors that say "All joking about blowing up the plane will be taken seriously." Life seemed a lot simpler when I was a kid.
—Gwen, mother of one, Kansas City, Missouri

Giving Your Child the Big Picture

Proportion of U.S. teenagers who say they fear being victimized: 24%

(Source: New York Times/*CBS News poll, 1999)*

Talking about our role in a violent world means that we need to question the term *innocent bystander.* Being an observer means that we are involved, for better or worse, when we come upon a violent situation. One of the goals of this talk is to get children to see that they, in many cases, have choices to make when they see a violent situation in progress. They may have the power to change a situation and help others. It's not always easy, and there are risks to intervening in a potentially violent situation. Perhaps your child could get special training in conflict resolution. Your school district office should have information on school safety courses for students. Whether or not a child feels she can actually intervene, she needs to know that in many violent situations observers do have the power to mediate conflict. She may feel too small and powerless to intervene today, but that can change as she gets bigger or becomes more confident, and acquires new skills and support.

I hear a lot about how people should get involved and stop violence. But what can a smaller child do when they see a bigger student or group of students threatening another student? I don't want my daughters to get hurt by getting involved.
—Karen, mother of two, Portland, Oregon

I've been very specific about what I want my sons to do if they see any kind of threats of violence at school. I don't want them to stand by

*and cheer on anybody. I don't want them getting hurt by trying to
break up a fight. I would like them to report anything immediately to
an adult. They both said they don't want to be known as the "guys
who report" because then they will be next on the list to be beat up.
This is complicated stuff to deal with when you are young.*
—Linda, mother of two, Memphis, Tennessee

When Do Observers Get Involved?

If you ask any kid when he might think about helping someone
who is being picked on, their first question asked is, "Do I know
the person who is being attacked?" Children, like adults, seem to
care about people when they know them. This makes sense. If we
cared about everyone who needed help, we might not be able to
walk down a busy city block without getting involved in a lot of
people's lives and problems. Still, there are those who have a very
strong internal sense of justice. When they see someone being
wronged, whether they know the person or not, they get involved. This is somewhat rare behavior. When asked afterward
why she acted as she did, a "good Samaritan" often says something
like "I couldn't stand there and not get involved." What's significant about the emotional makeup of such people are their deep
feelings of commitment and attachment to others. An internal
sense of justice is an important concept to address with children as
they observe small-scale injustices happening all around them.

*When I was in high school I was part of the band. We were considered
the geeks, and a lot of us were picked on by the jocks. We finally got
fed up with it. We decided to stand up for each other. One day a guy*

on the band got threatened by a jock who said he was going to get him after school—with help from his jock buddies, of course. After school nobody really talked about it, but about thirty of us from the band hung out with the guy who was threatened. We did that after school for a week. Each time the jocks showed up and saw our numbers they didn't say or do anything.—Sharon, New York City

I used to believe that when you see two guys fighting, it's between the two of them. It's like an unwritten code of manhood. But I don't want my son to be beaten to a pulp and have nobody come to his defense.
—Greg, father of two, Seattle, Washington

I know that when I was in high school and I thought about stopping a fight, I had a zillion thoughts run through my head: What would mom do? What would my pastor say? What will my brother tell everyone? What will my teacher do? Will I get in trouble? Will I get my face bashed in? I've got to admit, when I added up the pros and cons, I usually decided not to get involved.
—Polly, mother of two, Rockville, Maryland

Different Families: Different Values

Everyone interprets behaviors in his or her own way. Here are some behaviors that may be experienced differently depending on a person's background:

A boy starts shoving another boy outside school. A crowd of students forms a circle around them. One boy in the group steps in and says, "Hey, break it up."

Some parents call this "butting into other people's business." Others say "let the guys work it out themselves." Still others say it's important to stop all violent acts before anybody gets hurt. What do you think?

▪

A girl sitting with a group of her friends turns to a younger girl and calls her a slut. The younger girl's friend says, "Don't call my friend names. That's mean."

Some parents would say it's good to see friends stand up for each other. Others might feel that it's best just to ignore name-calling. What do you think?

▪

Two boys are walking down the hall. One of the boys grabs a girl's hips and the girl has to forcibly remove his hands. She pushes him away and the boy says, "You have sex with everyone, why not me?" The boy's best friend thinks it's a terrible thing to say, but he laughs anyway.

Some parents would say that the best friend didn't do anything wrong. Others might think he should have defended the girl by intervening. What do you think?

The situations above illustrate different ways people observe potentially violent situations. When faced with an altercation involving a schoolmate or friend, people have choices. How would your child react in similar situations if he were the observer?

Last-minute Checkups before the Talk

Before you begin the talk, take some time to ask yourself some questions.

- When you were a child, how did you feel about victims, victimizers, and observers? Were these terms you would have understood?
- When you were a child, did a parent tell you to break up a fight if you happened to see one? Or did they tell you to mind your own business?
- Did they tell you to stand up for people if others called them names?
- Did you ever discuss nonviolent ways to solve conflicts?

How do you think your childhood experiences have affected the way you're raising your child?

- Have you talked to your children about what to do when they see a fight?
- Are they supposed to stand up for someone who's called names at school, or stay out of it?
- Have you discussed nonviolent ways to solve conflicts?

Do you have any stories you can share with your child about stopping fights or preventing violence? For example:

- A time you broke up a fight between two people or saw someone break up a fight

- A time you were a victim of violence with other people watching
- A time you watched a fight and didn't do anything to help

Sharing your stories lets your child know you are human and that you too had challenges similar to the ones she has.

What Are Your Family Rules?

Do you have family rules about observing violence and other threatening behavior? If not, this is a good time to think about them. The talk outlined in this chapter highlights the following situations:

- Students watching a fight
- A boy watches an older guy harass a girl
- A girl watching a boy name-calling

Discussing these situations will give you an opportunity to discuss your family rules. What would you want your child to do in each situation? What are your expectations? Before the talk, think about what rules you want to communicate to your child. At the end of the talk, you will have the chance to review the rules with your child.

The Talk

Introduce the Talk

You can introduce this talk any way you like. What sounds like a good approach to some parents sounds contrived and unrealistic to others. You know your child and how best to secure some time for a talk. The following scenarios offer some options.

With this book in hand, you could tell your child: "I would like ten minutes of your time to talk about how to handle bullies at school."

A common response is "Again? We just talked about this stuff."

Your first talk should have prepared you for your child's reaction. Kids have an unending supply of excuses, and their imaginative rejections could fill a book.

You could say, "I'm reading a chapter about victimizers, victims, and observers. Do you have any ideas what these words might mean?"

Odds are, these are new terms for behaviors he is very familiar with.

You could say, "If a bigger guy was picking on a smaller guy and a bunch of students were watching, who is the victimizer? The victim? The observer?"

Review These Words

Please review the terms in this section. Discussing all the terms with your child is optional. You know what's appropriate for your child's age and maturity level. More than likely, even the youngest children have heard these words on TV.

conflict mediation: A nonviolent way of ending a conflict through talking. Example: If a person learns how to use conflict mediation, she learns how to keep people from fighting by helping them talk about their differences and the source of their anger. Some schools offer classes in conflict mediation.

observer: Someone who watches. Example: When students watch a fight between two guys, the people watching are called observers.

victim: Someone hurt or attacked by someone else. Example: When a boy hits or says mean things to another boy, the person who is hurt is the victim.

victimizer: Someone who makes a victim of someone else; someone who attacks or threatens another person. Example: When someone is picking on another student, he is a bully or a victimizer.

Why Is Talking about Roles Important?

Ask your child whether she thinks talking about roles is important. Here are some reasons you might want to offer:

- Talking about roles means learning to identify the victimizers, victims, and observers in any given situation.
- Talking about roles means learning to see how being a passive observer might contribute to violence or the threat of violence.
- Talking about roles means clarifying family rules about intervening in potentially violent situations.
- Talking about roles makes our family rules about being a victimizer more clear.

The Stories

In the next part of the talk, you'll be reading short stories to your child and discussing them together. You don't have to read all of the stories. Pick the ones that you think are appropriate for your child. The stories are very simple. Feel free to embellish them, adding details that you think might make the story more believable to your child.

The Story about Boys Fighting after School

This story provides an opportunity to discuss the roles of victim, victimizer, and observer.

"A girl is with a group of students watching a fight after school. A big boy has pushed a smaller boy and called him a name. It looks like the two boys are about to start hitting each other."

Ask these questions of your child:

- What is the girl thinking?
- What is the big guy thinking?
- What is the smaller guy thinking?
- Does the girl say anything?

Now that your child has completed this scenario, ask the following questions:

- What can happen to the girl if she tries to stop the fight?
- Do you think the two guys want to fight? If so, what might they be fighting about?
- Is this an example of a threat of violence? Why?

- Is this an example of violence? Why?
- What could the girl do to stop the fight?
- How often does someone stop a fight? How does a person stop it?
- Have you ever seen or been in a situation like this? If so, how did you feel? What did you do?

The Story about Girls Fighting after School

This story gives you a chance to discuss the roles of victim, victimizer, and observer. You may also compare and contrast it to the situation in the previous story.

"A boy is with a group of students watching what might become a fight after school. A big girl has called a smaller girl a cruel name. It looks like the bigger girl is going to grab the smaller girl."

Ask these questions of your child:

- What is the boy thinking?
- What is the big girl thinking?
- What is the smaller girl thinking?
- Does the boy say anything?

Now that your child has completed this scenario, ask the following questions:

- What can happen to the boy if he tries to stop the fight?
- Do you think the two girls want to fight? If so, what might they be fighting about?
- Is this an example of a threat of violence? Why?
- Is this an example of violence? Why?
- What could the boy do to stop the fight?
- How often does someone stop a fight? How does a person stop it?
- Have you ever seen or been in a situation like this? If so, how did you feel? What did you do?

Clarify Your Family's Values

Discuss these questions with your child as a way of sharing your values about behavior. A number of potential responses from children are included to help you formulate your own responses.

Ask your child: "When an observer sees a fight starting, what can he do?"

Child response #1: Nothing.
Parent: Nothing? It depends on the situation. The observer can make some important choices. Can the observer intervene without putting herself at risk? Can she try to get the people who are fighing to talk it out instead of punch it out?

Child response #2: Tell somebody.
Parent: Who can you tell? What can happen to you if you do that?

Child response #3: Get my friends to help me break it up.
Parent response: How can you do that?

The Story about Waiting for the Movie

This story gives you an opportunity to discuss how people can respond to harassment and threatening behavior.

"A teenage boy is in line waiting to buy a ticket for a movie. He spots a teenage girl in line who is being bothered by an older guy. She doesn't know the guy. The guy is standing very close to her and trying to start a conversation. She is backing away and trying to ignore him. Everyone else in line is ignoring the situation. The girl has asked the guy to leave her alone but he refuses."

Ask these questions of your child:

- What is the teenage boy who is watching thinking?
- What is the teenage girl thinking?
- What is the older guy thinking?
- What is the teenage boy who is watching saying?
- What is the teenage girl saying?

Now that your child has completed this scenario, ask the following questions:

- Why would the older guy be bothering the teenage girl?

- Is this an example of a threat of violence?
- Is this an example of violence?
- What should the boy who is watching do?
- What should the girl do?
- Have you seen or been in a situation like this? If so, how did you feel? What did you do?

Clarify Your Family's Values

Discuss these questions with your child as a way of sharing your values about behavior.

Ask your child: "What can someone do when they see someone being harassed, threatened, or about to be hit?"

Child response #1: Do nothing.
Parent: If someone older was bothering you, what kind of support would you like from people around you? If you need help getting away from the person, it would be good to have someone stick up for you on your behalf.

Child response #2: Yell, "stop!"
Parent: Yes. Yelling "stop" is a good idea. You also can try to get some other people to help you stand up for the potential victim. And you can try to get help from an adult.

Child response #3: It depends if you know the person who is being harassed or hit.
Parent: Whether you know the person or not, if you can help

without putting yourself at risk, I'd like you to try to stop any threatening behavior.

Parent: When does flirting become harassment? And when does harassment become intimidation or a threat of violence?

Child: Flirting isn't a threat. People like it. It's fun.

Parent: It all depends on the situation. Sometimes being flirted with feels nice. If a person is the object of flirting and feels uncomfortable, then there is a problem. Unwanted flirting might be viewed as harassment, intimidation, or a threat of violence.

The Story about Name-calling

This story is an opportunity to discuss the role of the observer.

"A girl is in the school hallway. She hears an older boy calling a younger boy some cruel names. The younger boy is very upset."

Ask these questions of your child:

- What is the girl thinking?
- What is the older boy thinking?
- What is the younger boy thinking?
- What is the girl saying?

Now that your child has completed this scenario, ask the following questions:

- How is this an example of the threat of violence?
- How is this an example of violence?
- What should the girl do?
- What should the younger boy do?
- Why would the older boy do something like that?
- What happens if the girl tells the older boy to stop and he doesn't?
- Have you ever seen or been in a situation like this? If so, how did you feel? What did you do?

Clarify Your Family's Values

Discuss these questions with your child as a way of sharing your values about behavior.

Ask your child: "When a person calls other people cruel names, what should you do?"

Child response #1: I don't know.
Parent: How would you like a person to help you if someone else was calling you cruel names?

Child response #2: It depends if I know the person.
Parent: Right. It depends on the situation. The person being called the names might be comfortable handling the situation by himself. He may also feel ashamed or threatened and just want to leave the situation.

The Bare Minimum: A Quick Quiz for Kids

Ask your child the following questions to assess her knowledge of the roles people play in violent situations.

1. Can you give me an example of how a person might go from being an observer to being a victim of violence?
   Sample answer:
   If a bully wants to beat up a student and you try to defend that student, the bully may turn his anger on you. You may find yourself in the role of the victim.

2. How can a person go from being a passive observer to being someone who intervenes in a fight?
   Sample answer:
   Usually it takes a very confident person to try to break up a fight. This confidence can come from being bigger than the bully or having training in conflict mediation. Often it takes some bravery to try to break up a fight, because the observer risks getting hurt.

Talk about Your Family Rules

This is an opportunity to review your family rules. Ask your child the follow questions.

1. What is our family rule about observing violent or threatening behavior?
   Sample answer:
   When you see people fighting, do not root them on.

2. What is our family rule about getting involved when we observe a violent situation?
   • When you see a violent or threatening situation, try to stop it if you can do so without putting yourself at risk.

- When you see a violent or threatening situation and you feel that you can't intervene, try to get help.
- When your friends are threatened, come to their defense as long as it does not put you at risk of harm or make a violent situation worse.

After the Talk

Parents are surprised by how much kids know about the roles in violent situations—roles that have many labels. Your goal is to help your child understand that she can play a role in making situations safer.

A Moment to Reflect

Take a moment to reflect on the talk you just had with your child. How do you feel about it?

- What surprised you about your child's perceptions of roles? Did he identify more with the role of observer, victimizer, or victim?
- Did your child see the observer as an innocent bystander?
- How much time did you spend listening to your child during the talk?
- Do you feel a need to read between the lines of his answers?

Warning Signs

The talks also may reveal potential problems your child is facing, whether in the role of the victim, victimizer, or observer. It's very common for children to act out during these talks, and an unresponsive child may just be having a bad day. However, there may be cause for concern if you hear from your child that

- he doesn't appear to care if students are hurt.
- she doesn't see anything wrong with calling others cruel names.
- he thinks people deserve to be hurt.
- he identifies strongly with the victimizers or victims in the stories.

Trust your instincts about how your child is doing. Learning to talk about these issues takes time. If you can't engage a younger child in any talks about these issues, consider asking for support from family members or trusted friends.

Finding Help

If needed, support and help for your child is available. Help comes in many forms. Your child, if he feels like a victim or an observer, may benefit from taking courses in self-defense or conflict mediation. For the victimizer, a course in anger management or some form of counseling may be helpful. Your child's school will have resources.

Success Stories

You have made it through talk number two. In the course of the talk, some children told stories about cheering on fights after school or passively watching small kids being bullied. But other kids shared stories about wanting to take conflict resolution classes, or what they've learned in violence prevention classes. One dad in

Philadelphia, Pennsylvania, said the talk was a great opportunity to talk with his son, who'd been aggressive with other kids, about other ways to express his anger.

But no matter what your child shared, you're continuing a vital process. Your child has a new vocabulary to describe violent situations and her role in them. And she has a parent willing to take the time to listen.

Sample Talks

Between Parents and Children

If you are wondering how a talk based on this chapter might really sound, take a look at the following excerpts from real family talks.

Discussing the Story about Boys Fighting after School

Participants: a mother and her seventh-grade son.

Mom: This is a story about a group of students watching a fight after school. One big guy and a smaller guy are going to fight. One girl is watching. Now, what is the girl thinking when this fight is going to start?

Child: You want to know what the girl is thinking?

Mom: Yes.

Child: She thinks this is going to be cool.

Mom: This is going to be cool?

Child: Yeah.

Mom: What is the big guy thinking when he is starting the fight?

Child: He thinks he's going to win.

Mom: What is the smaller guy thinking?

Child: He thinks he has a pretty good chance, but he might lose.

Mom: Okay, what does the girl who is observing say?

Child: "Come on, let's go. Good job, let's go."

Mom: Why is she saying that?

Child: 'Cause she's really into this. If she came after school, she's not going home, so she must be interested in it.

Mom: Okay. What can happen to the girl if she tries to stop the fight?

Child: She'll get ignored.

Mom: Okay, is this an example of violence? Why?

Child: Yes, 'cause they are fighting.

Mom: Is this an example of a threat of violence? Why?

Child: No, they aren't threatening anyone.

Mom: They are just threatening each other?

Child: They are fighting.

Mom: They are actually fighting, so that's not a threat?

Child: Yeah.

Mom: How many times a year do you think this kind of thing happens in your school?

Child: Uh, like around five or ten times.

Mom: Have you ever seen a situation like this?

Child: Yeah.

Mom: What did you do when you saw them fighting?

Child: I watched.

Mom: Did anyone do anything about it?

Child: No. Well, the teachers, eventually.

Lessons Learned from This Sample Talk

The child may find the role of observer satisfying. The parent may wish to talk about how the child might feel if he were the victim. This may be time for the parent to mention that cheering on a fight encourages violence. Often, a bully is looking for an audience, so merely observing a fight can escalate violence. The parent might also ask: How do you feel being an observer? If no one watched would the people still fight?

Discussing the Story about Waiting for the Movies

Participants: a father and his third-grade daughter.

Dad: A boy is waiting in line at the movies. He sees a girl in line. She is being bothered by an older guy. She doesn't know the older guy. Tell me what you think the girl is thinking.

Daughter: She thinks that this guy is not going away.

Dad: What do you think the older guy is thinking?

Daughter: He thinks, "I'm going to try to get this girl to like me."

Dad: What do you think the boy is thinking? The boy who is watching.

Daughter: I think he's trying to ignore it. He just wants to see the movie.

Dad: Okay, so what is the girl saying?

Daughter: "Leave me alone."

Dad: Why would the older guy bother the girl?

Daughter: He is stupid.

Dad: Is this an example of a threat of violence?

Daughter: Um, yeah. In some ways. I know what I would do.

Dad: What?

Daughter: I would say, "You'd better get away from me! I'll give you a big crunch (she makes a fist) if you don't."

Dad: What should the boy who is watching do?

Daughter: He should try to protect the girl.

Dad: Have you ever been in a situation like that? Or something like that?

Daughter: I've been threatened. Some boy at school was bothering me for some candy.

Dad: And what did you do?

Daughter: Well, I yelled for my friend.

Dad: Oh? Did that work?

Daughter: Of course.

Lessons Learned from This Sample Talk

This parent found out a number of things. His daughter did not think a girl should be bothered by the older guy and she thought that the observer should help. This suggests an internal sense of justice which could be nurtured in future discussions. She also thought threatening the guy with "a big crunch" was an acceptable response to the guy's advances. The father could further probe into how realistic it is for a girl to physically threaten an older guy and what other options exist when dealing with a harasser. He also found out that his daughter has been harassed at school and seemed to be able to handle herself in that situation. He might ask his daughter how she felt when she was threatened at school by the boy, and what she might do if a friend isn't around when she is being bothered.

Discussing the Story about Name-calling

Participants: a mother and her fifth-grade son.

Mom: This is a story about some kids playing at school. A girl hears some bigger guy calling a smaller student some cruel names. Is this an example of a threat of violence, if one boy is yelling bad names to the other boy?

Child: No, not really. It's like neither because he's not hitting him or doing violent things. He's insulting someone.

Mom: And that's different from threatening with violence?

Child: Yes. And if he says, "I'm going to beat you up or else" . . . something like that, then that's a threat.

Mom: Okay. What should the girl do?

Child: Tell a teacher.

Mom: Have you ever seen or been in a situation like this?

Child: No.

Lessons Learned from This Sample Talk

The parent and child have explored the concept of name-calling as a threat of violence. The parent may wish to discuss how some name-calling can feel like a threat of violence to the victim. It might be helpful for the parent to clarify when a child should get help from an adult and when it might be appropriate to stand up for someone who is being called names. The child said he had never seen name-calling. Statistics make this unlikely, and future talks might reveal the child's experience with name-calling situations. The parent might ask: How do you feel about name-calling? How do you think it feels to be called a name?

3

Patterns of Force

Talking about Violence in the Home

The family is not the unlikeliest place for violence—it is the likeliest. It is the place with the most repeated provocations and the place where many people show the least self-control and the most sense of entitlement. It has to be our first teaching ground and our first line of defense against attitudes, habits and grudges that go on to terrorize our entire society.
—Pepper Schwartz, Ph.D., University of Washington

Families are the primary incubators of violence today, as they have always been.—Richard Rhodes, author of *Why They Kill: The Discoveries of a Maverick Criminologist*

I grew up in a big family with lots of brothers. The bad news was that I was picked on all the time at home. The good news was that they protected me from everybody else.
—Ray, taxi driver, Kansas City, Missouri

Irun workshops on parent-child communication, and an important part of my work is traveling around the country, meeting with parents and hearing about the struggles they're facing. In April 1999, two students in Littleton, Colorado, opened fire on their classmates at a school called Columbine High, and in the weeks that followed, I found myself extraordinarily busy. In one month I met with families in Dalton, Georgia; in South Dakota's Pine Ridge Indian Reservation; and in Kansas City, San Antonio, Memphis, and Jamestown, New York.

The people I met ranged across a wide spectrum, from families living below the poverty level to others who were comfortably middle-class. Their concerns were diverse. But one topic stood out: violence. In those weeks after Columbine, parents everywhere were asking themselves how the families of the two gunmen could have overlooked their kids' warning signs. The parents I met spoke in English, Spanish, and Lakota, but their words were the same: "How can I improve communication with my child? How can we make our children's world safer?"

The Columbine tragedy has produced a national soul searching, and many people are finding that the search leads to their front door. The parents in my workshops are taking a sober look at how safe their child's home life is, and what kinds of role models their kids have at home.

Preparing for the Talk

Talking about violence in the home can produce a lively debate within families. Your child might see this talk as his chance to banish discipline from his world (It isn't). Of all the talks, this is one that needs to be carried out with the greatest sensitivity.

The goal of this talk is to make your child feel safe in her home. As with all the talks, potentially violent situations are discussed. However, because these examples center on home life, they have the ability to unsettle a child. As with all the talks, feel free to pick and choose the portions of the talk that you feel are appropriate for your child.

Violent behavior can visit homes in a variety of forms, from brothers fighting over a new toy to parents striking each other. But even in the most peaceful families, the talk on violence at home is necessary for a number of reasons. First, it's normal for young children to experiment with a certain amount of roughhousing, accompanied by name-calling and threats. Violence also enters the home through the TV, Internet, and other media, all of which expose children to stories about child victimization, spousal abuse, beatings, murders, incest, and sexual abuse. Also, even if your home is relatively violence free, children may hear about violence occuring in the homes of relatives. Talking about these terms, in language appropriate for your child, will help her understand why these things happen and how to identify potentially violent situations that may occur in the home.

In this talk you will help your child understand that

- he can depend on you for support when facing any kind of violence from a family member or visitor in your home.
- you have expectations about his behavior at home.
- there are family rules about violence and safety at home.

What You Can Expect from This Talk

After this talk your child will:

- be able to identify threats of violence or violent behavior in the home.
- understand the importance of respecting other members of the household.
- understand the family rules about violence and safety in the home.
- know where to go for help if problems with a family member arise.

What's Acceptable in Your Home?

Parents differ greatly in their views on physical aggression in the home. Is physical discipline a small act of violence? Should two brothers fight each other in the backyard? Should a sister slam a door in her younger brother's face? Should a grandparent threaten to punish a grandson for breaking a plate? It's up to you to maintain a safe home environment and to make your own decisions about what behavior you will accept in your home.

To prepare for the talk, think back to your childhood and how you perceived any acts of violence or threats of violence in the home. Consider the reflections of the following parents as they look back on their childhood home life with mixed feelings.

My mother always said that if Dad had hit her even once, she would pack up and leave—and take us with her, of course.
—Suzanne, mother of three, Denver, Colorado

The police were always coming to our neighbors' house because of the fights. My parents wouldn't let me play with the neighbor kids—even though we were friends—because of their parents.
—Stacy, mother of two, Yakima, Washington

My older brother was always violent. It got worse when my mother went back to work. I felt it was my responsibility to stand up to him and protect my little sister. I couldn't tell my mom because she would feel guilty when working made her happy. I couldn't tell my dad because he might get so angry as to lose control and hurt my brother. I wouldn't have admitted what was going on to anybody. I might have told my parents if I had seen that they would deal with the situation calmly and without becoming really angry.
—Samantha, Seattle, Washington

When I was a kid I dreaded weekends. Every Friday night, like clockwork, my mom started hurling insults at my dad. And by Saturday my dad was hitting my mom. This ritual went on for years in front of me and my brother and sister.—Andrew, father of two, New York City

Influence of the Media

What does your child know about violence in the home? If he watches TV, he has been exposed to movies and news programs about child abuse, incest, spousal abuse, and physical and verbal aggression between siblings. He has seen films or videos about violent dads or gun-toting boyfriends who make the house a prison for the moms, girlfriends, and kids. Occasionally a female is seen terrorizing the home with intimidation and an ax. How does a child interpret these images of violence in the home? What your child thinks is, in some ways, determined by what she has viewed in the media. In the course of the talk, you may be able to find out what the media has taught your child about violence in the home.

Pressure to Keep Quiet

It's not uncommon for children to think that their families are the only families with problems. From the outside, other families seem okay. Most children don't want to lose face or be embarrassed by revealing any personal problems that are occurring in the home—whether they have to do with alcohol, drugs, money, or violence. If you experienced violence or threats of violence in your home when you were a child, did you talk about it? How comfortable were you discussing it with someone you trusted? What kind of support did you find?

After years of emotional abuse, when I was in high school I finally broke down and called my aunt to talk about the threats my mother was making. She offered supportive words over the phone. A few months later I was visiting her and my older cousins. I asked what I could do about my family situation. She pulled me aside and said, "We don't talk about those things in front of other family members." I never asked for help again from anyone.
—Donna, mother of one, New York City

I didn't realize how dysfunctional my family was until I was in high school and started visiting other families. Up until then I thought that

threats, cruel comments, and intimidation was what all parents did.
—Pam, mother of two, Rockville, Maryland

Giving Your Child the Big Picture

Those of us who treasure our children find it incomprehensible that any parent could hurt a child. But the data suggests that violence at home is a major social problem.

Proportion of child murder victims who are killed by a family member: 22%

(Source: U.S. Office of Juvenile Justice and Delinquency Prevention, 1997)

Why are family members violent toward each other? This is a question you can expect from your child during this talk. This is a good time to reassure your child that your job is to create a home that is safe, secure, and free from violent behavior. You will want to reassure your child that if there is violence in a home, there are people who can help. Police, counselors, social workers, and other family members can step in to help a family member who is being violent or threatening others.

My Aunt Patty was like having another parent. She was always around to talk to, like a trusted friend. When my older brother started bossing me around and hitting me, she stepped in and let him know that he couldn't get away with it.—Peter, father of two, Chicago, Illinois

I don't think any young child can understand why incest or sexual abuse happens. But it's important that they understand that some-times it does happen—and that it's very wrong.
—Rachel, mother of three, Dalton, Georgia

Some parents send very mixed messages about violence. Parents who use threats of violence often raise children who threaten. Children learn by modeling the behavior of their parents. The following quotes illustrate parents with good intentions but using language, and possibly behaviors, that may have been doing more harm than good.

I tell my kids that I'm going to whip 'em so they know right from wrong. This will keep them from getting into situations where the police might whip 'em.—Jamie, mother of three, Atlanta, Georgia

I came home one day after being beaten up by two guys after school. My dad was furious. He had sent me to a Catholic school to avoid such problems. He said, "Nobody should be laying a hand on you. I'm gonna find those boys and beat the hell out of them."
—Cliff, father of one, New York City

Different Families: Different Values

Everyone defines acceptable home behavior in his or her own way. Here are some behaviors that may be experienced differently depending on a person's background:

An older brother threatens to hit his sister.

Some families see this as normal, while others forbid even a threat of violence.

■

A father threatens to slug his teenage son if he doesn't finish his chores.

Some view this as a father's right and duty, while others see this threat of violence as inappropriate. Some parents use ways other than threats of violence to show anger or disapproval.

■

While a boy listens from his bedroom, the mother's new boyfriend tells her, "Shut your mouth or I'll shut it for you."

Some might excuse this statement as a joke, or something said in the heat of anger. Others view this kind of language as disrespectful and inappropriate. It can be viewed as a real threat and a warning sign of potential violence.

Last-minute Checkups before the Talk

Before you talk to your child, think about your experience with violence in the home when you were growing up.

- When you were a child, did you feel safe from physical violence at home?
- Could you talk with a parent about any problems related to violence?
- Did you have clear family rules about violence and safety?
- Did anyone in your home express anger with physical aggression?

Do you think your child's experiences are very different from your experiences growing up?

- Do you think your child feels safe from physical violence in your home?
- If your child felt threatened, do you think she would be able to discuss it with you?
- Do you have clear family rules about violence and safety?

This is a good time to think about your first experiences with violence in the home as a child. Do you have any stories that you can share with your child? For example:

- Watching a relative hit someone
- Dealing with a threatening sibling or family member
- Confronting a potential abuser in the home

Sharing your childhood stories with your child can be a very rich and useful experience.

What Are Your Family Rules?

Do you have family rules about violence in the home? If not, this is a good time to think about them. The talk outlined in this chapter highlights the following situations:

- A dad angry with his son
- An older sister angry with her brother
- A mom and dad fighting in front of the kids

Before you have your talk about violence in the home, consider spending some time reviewing the family rules you have in place. Are your rules working? It's important that your child have a clear understanding of the rules, why they are put in place, and the consequences of breaking them. At the end of the talk you will be able to review all the family rules about violence and safety at home with your child.

The Talk

Introduce the Talk

With this book in hand, tell your child: "I'd like to talk with you about keeping safe at home."

By now you most likely have figured out the best way to secure five minutes to talk with your child. Your child most likely can recite the following line for you. "It's part of my job as a parent to have this talk, and it's part of your job as my child to participate."

You could say, "What are some examples of violence that can happen in the home?"

After identifying some examples, such as when family members yell, hit, fight, push, name-call, or slap, you may proceed with the next section.

Review These Words

Please review the terms in this section. Discussing all the terms with your child is optional. You know what's appropriate for your child's age and maturity level. More than likely, even the youngest children have heard these words on TV.

child abuse: verbal or physical maltreatment or cruelty directed at a child by an older person

discipline: rules governing conduct

domestic partner abuse: verbal and/or physical maltreatment or cruelty between adults who are living together in an intimate relationship, whether opposite or same sex

emotional abuse: treating a person in a way that is cruel. Deliberately causing emotional pain, hurt, or neglect

family counselor: a person who can provide help to families with problems

incest: sexual activity between close family members

sexual abuse: any kind of unwanted touching of a sexual nature, or unwanted sexual contact

spousal abuse: verbal and/or physical maltreatment or cruelty between a husband and a wife

unsafe touching: the kind of touching that makes a person feel uncomfortable

Note: Unsafe touching is an important term to discuss, especially for younger children. One approach is to say something like the following: "Sometimes a person might touch your knee or shoulder in such a way that makes you feel scared. Sometimes a person might try to touch your private parts (chest, below your belly button and anyplace around your underwear). This is not a place any person should be touching. You control your body and who can touch it. You have permission to yell or run away from anyone (adult, friend, or family member) if you feel that they are trying to touch you in any unsafe way. Sometimes it's difficult to know when touching is unsafe. You should always let a parent know if you think you've been touched in an unsafe way."

Why Is Talking about Violence in the Home Important?

Ask your child whether she thinks talking about violence in the home is important. Here are some reasons you might want to offer:

- I know sometimes there are problems with your siblings, and I want to know about it.
- I want to make sure you know the rules and the consequences of breaking them.
- I want you to know that even though you might see threatening behavior in other people's homes, it's not okay in ours.

The Stories

In the next part of the talk, you'll be reading short stories to your child and discussing them together. You don't have to read all of the stories. Pick the ones that you think are appropriate for your child. The stories are very simple. Feel free to embellish them, adding details that you think might make the story more believable to your child.

The Story about a Boy and His Dad

This story provides an opportunity to discuss how parents might express anger.

"A boy has just done something to

make his dad very angry (You can make up anything you want). Dad is yelling at his son."

Here are some suggestions why the dad might be angry: The son left the lawnmower outside in the rain, brought the car home with no gas in it, downloaded a file containing a virus, broke something, or is behaving in a way the dad doesn't approve of.

Ask these questions of your child:

- What is the dad saying?
- What is the son saying?
- What is the dad thinking?
- What is the son thinking?

Now that your child has completed this scenario, ask the following questions:

- What did the son do to anger his dad?
- Might the dad become violent?
- What would stop the dad from becoming violent?
- What's a nonviolent way for the dad to express his anger?
- Has anything like this ever happened to you or to a friend?
- If so, how did you feel? What did you or your friend do?
- How would this situation be different if it was the mother who was angry with the son? Or if the mother was angry with the daughter?

Follow up with any questions that you feel are appropriate given your child's responses.

The Story about a Big Sister and Little Brother

This story gives you a chance to discuss threats of violence between siblings.

"A sister is baby-sitting her younger brother. She is very angry because of something her brother just did (You can make up anything you want). The sister is yelling at her brother."

Ask these questions of your child:

- What is the sister saying?
- What is the brother saying?
- What is the sister thinking?
- What is the brother thinking?

Now that your child has completed this scenario, ask the following questions:

- What did the boy do to anger his sister?
- Might the sister want to hit her brother?
- What would stop the sister from hitting her brother?
- What's a nonviolent way for the sister to express her anger?
- Has anything like this ever happened to you or to a friend?
- If so, how did you feel? What did you or your friend do?
- How would this situation be different if it were an older brother baby-sitting a younger sibling?

Follow up with any questions that you feel are appropriate given your child's responses.

The Story about Mom, Dad, and the Kids

This story gives you an opportunity to discuss threats of violence between parents.

"A dad and mom are angry at each other. They are yelling at each other about money and bills. The kids are watching from the living room."

Ask these questions of your child:

• What is the dad thinking?
• What is the mom thinking?
• What is the brother thinking?
• What is the sister thinking?

Now that your child has completed this scenario, ask the following questions:

• What are the mom and dad fighting about?
• How does the mom feel?
• How does the dad feel?
• How do the kids feel?
• Could the mom and dad hurt each other emotionally or physically?
• What are nonviolent ways for the mom and dad to express their anger?
• Has anything like this ever happened to you or a friend?
• If so, how did you feel? What did you or your friend do?

Follow up with any questions that you feel are appropriate given your child's responses.

> *When I was in the navy and I was beat up I would have shot the guy who was hitting me if I had had a gun. I wanted justice. I was angry at society. Later, I learned he had been caught and tried. But the episode made me into a different kind of person. I'm raising sons who know hitting is unacceptable behavior and revenge does not equal justice. And I am glad I do not have to live my life knowing I had shot someone in one angry moment.*
> —Delores, mother of four, Costa Mesa, California

Clarify Your Family's Values

Discuss these questions with your child as a way of sharing your values about violence in the home. A number of potential responses from children are included to help you formulate your own responses.

Parent: If someone in the house was threatening you, what could you do? (This might be a friend of an older sibling, or an older relative or babysitter.)

Child: Run away from the person.

Parent: Yes, getting away from any threatening person is a good idea, even if this person is someone you thought you could trust. I want to hear about any threats from anyone in this house. My job is to keep this house safe.

Parent: How do you think parents decide what their family rules about violence and safety in the home will be?

Child: I don't know.

Parent: It's based on our background, our values, and fairness. Every family has its own rules. Some don't have any rules. If you were a parent, how would you make up rules to keep your child safe?

Parent: What are the consequences of breaking family rules?

Child: I don't know.

Parent: Every family has different rules and different consequences for breaking them. Some families take away privileges like TV or ask kids to take time out in their rooms. For breaking big rules a child might be grounded for a long time.

The Bare Minimum: A Quick Quiz for Kids

Ask your child the following questions to assess her knowledge of violence in the home.

1. Can you give me examples of violent behavior in the home? Sample answers:
- Pushing, shoving, or hitting anyone in the house
- Threatening to hurt anyone in the house
- Playing games or roughhousing that results in someone getting hurt

2. Why do you think some family members hit each other? Sample answers:
- They are roughhousing, and haven't been taught any differently
- They are angry at each another, and don't know any other way to express their anger

- This is their way of dealing with frustration and anger, which may or may not have anything to do with the family member
- This is how they were raised

Talk about Your Family Rules

This is an opportunity to review your family rules. Ask your child what your family rules about violence in the home are.

1. What are our family rules about violence in the home?
   Sample answers:
- We don't hit others
- We don't threaten others
- We don't slam doors on people
- If we are angry with someone we wait until we calm down and then discuss it

2. What are the consequences of breaking the family rules about violence in the home?
   Sample answers:
- Time out
- Being grounded
- No TV
- No friends in the house
- No access to the computer for fun
- No private phone calls

After the Talk

After the talk about violence in the home, many parents report learning more about their child's life, fears, thoughts, and ethics.

Some parents were surprised to hear about incidents between siblings and family members that they didn't know about. Others found that even the smallest child can have definite views about what's right and wrong.

A Moment to Reflect

Take a moment to reflect on the talk you just had with your child.

- Do you feel that your child is feeling safe and secure in the home? Were you concerned about anything you heard?
- Did you feel that your child was able to articulate his feelings or fears?
- Do you feel that you have family rules in place that keep your child safe? Are you comfortable enforcing the rules?
- How much of the time do you think you spent listening to your child?

Warning Signs

The talks also may reveal potential problems your child has with a family member. There may be cause for concern if you hear from your child that

- he doesn't appear to care if his siblings hurt him.
- she doesn't see anything wrong with calling family members cruel names.
- he thinks some family members deserve to be hurt.
- he reveals strong hostility toward family members in the stories.

Use your intuition. Your child may just be having a bad day when you try to talk about violence in the home. Using sarcasm or being unresponsive may be your child's way of acting out. But if the same warning signs appear talk after talk, you may want to consider seeking outside help with someone trained to deal with these matters.

Finding Help

If this talk revealed what you consider to be a serious problem, you may want to consider talking with a trusted family friend or a trained counselor or therapist. Many families need help from time to time. It often takes time and energy to find the right kind of assistance, but there are resources available.

Success Stories

Talk number three has been accomplished. Excellent work! For some families, this has been a difficult talk. One mom in Yakima, Washington, said she was in tears even before the talk, as she thought back on her own painful family life—but was heartened when she realized what a happy home she was now heading. A dad in Kansas City, Missouri, said he heard about sibling fights he never knew occurred; during the talk, he told his son he had higher expectations than that. Whether you felt the news your child gave you was good, bad, or a combination of both, take heart that you now have a better understanding of how safe your child feels in your home.

Sample Talks

Between Parents and Children

If you are wondering how a talk based on this chapter might really sound, take a look at the following excerpts from real family talks.

The Story about a Boy and His Dad

Participants: a mother and her seventh-grade son. In this family, the father and son had recently had an argument over whether the son could let a neighbor illegally copy a computer game.

Mom: This is a story about a boy and his dad. The boy wants to lend his computer game to a friend and the friend said he'd pay him to borrow the game. The dad is upset because he doesn't want him to loan out the game. Why doesn't he want him to?

Child: Because he thinks . . . because he doesn't trust the neighbors.

Mom: What does he think they're going to do with it?

Child: Steal the serial number.

Mom: And why does that upset him?

Child: It's illegal.

Mom: Okay. How is the dad feeling?

Child: Pissed off.

Mom: How is the boy feeling?

Child: Ticked off.

Mom: Might Dad want to get violent?

Child: No.

Mom: Why?

Child: (sarcastically) He's a Quaker or something, I don't know.

Mom: What's a nonviolent way for Dad to express his anger?

Child: Punish the son.

Mom: Punish his son?

Child: I don't know, just tell him he can't go outside to play and he's got to come inside for dinner, and then everything's fine because they have pumpkin pie and a good dinner made by their mom.

Mom: Okay. Has anything like this ever happened to you or to a friend?

Child: Gee, maybe (laughing).

Mom: So, what happened?

Child: I got really angry, and I just wanted to take the disk and sneak it over to my friend so he could copy it without anybody knowing about it.

Mom: Because you didn't agree with your father?

Child: I don't.

Mom: Okay, but did you understand why Dad just didn't want to get involved in that whole thing?

Child: Why?

Mom: Because he didn't want you involved in someone else's illegal activity.

Child: It wasn't illegal.

Mom: So you don't think it's illegal and he does?

Lessons Learned from This Sample Talk

Shortly after this talk the mother found her son to continue their conversation. She had become concerned over her son's admission that he would sneak the disk to his friend if he thought he could get away with it. In their follow-up talk, the mother discusses the importance of honesty, integrity, and following the family rules. The son's comment about dad being "a Quaker" illustrates how he uses sarcasm to express his anger. This is something the mother might consider pointing out. The parent might ask: Was the dad in this story threatening in any way? How did the son feel when he was being talked to by the father?

Discussing the Story about a Big Sister and Little Brother

Participants: a mom and her fourth-grade daughter.

Mom: I'm going to read a story about a big sister and a little brother. A younger brother has just done something to make his sister very angry. You can make up anything you want. Whatever he did, it made his sister very, very angry. The older sister is yelling at her brother. What do you think the boy is thinking?

Child: "I'm probably going to be hurt by her."

Mom: What do you think the sister is thinking?

Child: I think she's really mad that her brother did something.

Mom: What is the sister saying?

Child: "Don't do that!"

Mom: Well, good. And what is the brother saying?

Child: "Sorry, I'm really sorry."

Mom: Okay. What do you think the brother did to anger his sister?

Child: I think he took something of hers.

Mom: How do you think the sister is feeling about that?

Child: She's really kind of sad and mad.

Mom: And how is the brother feeling?

Child: He's feeling kind of scared.

Mom: Do you think the sister might want to hit her brother?

Child: Yes, probably.

Mom: What would keep her from hitting him?

Child: Do you mean, What would make her stop?

Mom: Yes.

Child: Probably if he did something really nice for his sister.

Mom: Like what? If he stole something from her and she wants to hit him and she's getting ready to hit him, what would make her stop?

Child: Can the mom stop her?

Mom: The mom? Yes, if the mom is there she can stop the sister from hitting. What's a nonviolent way for the sister to express her anger?

Child: Just ignore it?

Mom: Uh-huh. But if she needs to express her anger what can she do?

Child: She can just be mad?

Mom: Yes. Has anything like this ever happened to you or to a friend?

Child: Well, I don't know.

Mom: Have you ever taken anything from your brother?

Child: No, but he's taken money from me.

Mom: What did you do when he took money from you?

Child: I grabbed his arm. I tried to chase him and Dad just stopped him and I got my money back.

Lessons Learned from This Sample Talk

The parent may choose to discuss how family members can express anger in a way that is nonviolent. Bottling up or "ignoring" (as the daughter describes it) anger may not be healthy. The mom can talk about how some people may hide their anger for a long time and then when the pressure gets to be too much, the person might explode with rage and violence. The two can discuss parent-approved ways to express anger that are healthy, such as calmly stating the cause of the upset, punching a pillow, writing in a journal, or yelling in the shower. The parent might ask: How did you feel when your brother took your money?

Discussing the Story about Mom, Dad, and the Kids

Participants: a father and mother talk with their fourth-grade daughter.

Dad: This is a story about a dad and mom who are angry at each other. They are yelling at each other about money and bills. The kids are listening from the living room. What is the dad thinking?

Child: I think he's thinking angry thoughts.

Mom: What do you think the mom is thinking about?

Child: I think the mom is thinking about money and bills.

Dad: If mommy and I were arguing about money and bills, what do you think your little brother would be thinking about?

Child: Um, he probably would be worried that we don't have enough money.

Mom: Really? What would you think?

Child: I would be a little worried, because you might get divorced because of this.

Mom: Really?

Child: Yes. And I would be afraid we wouldn't be able to afford things and be really poor. I'd just be afraid.

Mom: How do you think the mom feels when they get angry and yell at each other?

Child: Well, it depends on how the mom is. 'Cause some mothers would care and some mothers wouldn't.

Dad: Do you think the mom and dad in the story could maybe hurt each other emotionally or physically?

Child: Not physically. But by what you were saying.

Mom: What are better ways for Mom and Dad to express their anger?

Child: Just by going back, cooling off, coming back, and talking it out. When you're all cooled down.

Mom: Has anything like this ever happened to you?

Child: No.

Mom: Have you ever heard of anything like the story happening to a friend?

Child: I don't know. I don't ask people those kinds of questions. I think those are personal questions.

Lessons Learned from This Sample Talk

It's interesting what a little story can bring up. This talk brought up divorce, the fear of being poor, and a young girl's belief that asking "those kinds of questions" about violence is personal and something she would not do. Further talks could explore re-specting personal boundaries and the privacy of others versus the need to be able to talk about a violent situation with someone outside of the family. The child has great ideas about non-violent ways to deal with anger by "cooling off, coming back, and talk-ing it out." The parent can ask: How does it feel when you "cool off?" When was the last time you felt the need to "cool off?"

4

What's the Message?

Talking about Violence in the Media

*If you are worried about what your kid eats, you should worry about
what your kid is watching.*
—Robert Lichter, president, Center for Media and Public Affairs

*I finally gave in and got my son the computer game he'd been
begging me to buy. One day I watched him play it, and I realized the
entire game consisted of nothing but killing—in an hour he must
have killed four-hundred simulated people. That was my first and
last purchase of a game like that.*
—Audrey, mother of two, Seattle, Washington

*I read that parents should think about taking the TV out of their
kids' rooms and just having one in the living room. At first I thought
that seemed a little drastic. Now that I've been watching how gory
cable and video are, I think it's a great idea.*
—Shelley, mother of three, Orlando, Florida

The nature and degree of violence in the media has been and will
continue to be the subject of debate in society. Researchers,
policy makers, industry representatives, and politicians do not always
agree—much less communicate with each other about these issues.
A few facts, however, are recognized by most people, though their

interpretation of the facts is likely to vary: Children are a special audience, media influences perceptions of reality, and violence in the media validates violence as conflict resolution.

The connection between viewing violence on TV or in films and the actual expression of violence continues to be debated and discussed by everyone—from the president of the United States to the American Academy of Pediatrics. But the debate that may affect you most directly is the one between you and your child on a Friday night at the video store. He might want to rent "Death Assassins Part 5," but you might wish he would stick to gentle cartoons. Even without definitive research establishing the direct link between simulated violence and the real thing, you may decide that it's not the healthiest idea for your child to have a media diet of shootings, torture, mutilations, and images of women being stalked. The media that surrounds you and your child conveys a set of values about how people should be treated, and these values may be very different from yours.

Believe it or not, a talk about media can actually engage a child. Talking about the latest TV show or movie is a topic young people can relate to. How you frame this talk may introduce a new way of talking about actors, scripts, plots, and special effects.

When it comes to the media, most Americans are bombarded from the day they are born. By the age of 18, it is estimated that the average U.S. child will have witnessed over 200,000 violent acts on TV, including at least 16,000 murders. As many children grow, popular music, electronic games, and films supplement a steady diet of TV—all with more messages about violence. Entertainment blends with news programs and popular magazines, shaping our attitudes about the prevalence and causes of violence. Of course, the mass media also contains programming which can enlighten, engage, and educate families about the world. There are many clear, helpful messages as well as mixed messages for your child to ponder.

Preparing for the Talk

This chapter will help you talk with your child about media messages and your family's values about the media's portrayal of violence against women, men, and children.

In this talk you will help your child understand that

- all media, including TV, films, music, and electronic games, contain messages.
- messages about violence in the media may affect people's attitudes and behaviors.
- the media portrays violent behavior and the consequences of violence in ways that often differ from real life.

What You Can Expect from This Talk

After the talk your child will

- have the ability to identify threats of violence or violent behavior in the media.
- understand how the media's messages can affect people's attitudes about violence—and how advertisers use violent images to sell movies, toys, and electronic games.
- understand your values and beliefs about violence in the media.

• understand your family rules about viewing violence in the media.

Who Is Being Hurt?

Chapter Two focused on talking about the roles people play: victim, victimizer, and observer. To fully understand the messages about violence on TV and film, we need to look at who Hollywood casts as the victims. In the most simplistic terms, Hollywood's action blockbusters tend to give us one handsome guy with a license to kill, and a lot of males to maim, shoot, or torture. Females, if included in any significant way, are often portrayed as vulnerable. What often spurs the hero into action is the killing of the "helpless" female. What kind of message does that send to a young boy or girl?

In all fairness, many alternatives to action films and TV shows exist. You can monitor much of what your child views. You can also make sure that you are familiar with the values being communicated through your child's favorite TV shows and films. It just makes a parent's job more difficult when the highly effective Hollywood marketing machine hypes an action film, sending ripple effects into advertising and general programming.

What We Watch Versus How We Watch Violence

Violence in the media is not going away. However, your family rules about TV and film viewing can help control both the flow and—perhaps more important—your child's interpretation of most of it. It's not realistic to ask every parent and child to stop watching all violent programming on TV. Many parents feel that a small dose of a shoot-'em-up with the accompanying adrenaline rush feels fine. The goal is to give your child the skills to watch violent programming critically, being aware of the way people are portrayed as victims, victimizers, observers, and heroes.

You can help teach your child to view television critically rather than passively. Try playing the role of movie critic with your child, pointing out plot holes, weak character development, stereotypical roles of males and females (or the absence of females), and how violence is used. You can also teach your child to view news and information programming with a critical eye.

I took my seventh grader to see Saving Private Ryan. *It was filled with lots of violence that showed a realistic war. And it was part of our history. After the movie we talked about how horrible war is.*
—Sandra, mother of two, Rockville, Maryland

I remember reading about Tipper Gore trying to get the music industry to offer parental warnings and a rating system on all CDs and tapes. When I was in my twenties it didn't seem important. I thought it was just another form of censorship. Now that I'm a mom with a teenager I really see how helpful the ratings are.
—Cindy, mother of one, Seattle, Washington

I am the official censor in our home and this does not make me popular with my thirteen-year-old son. He would rent slasher films every night if he could. He saw one movie that gave him nightmares for two weeks and he still wants to see this horror stuff.
—Lisa, mother of three, Memphis, Tennessee

What Do We Know about Violence in the Media?

Violent programs on television lead to aggressive behavior by children and teenagers who watch those programs. That's the word from a 1982 report by the National Institute of Mental Health, a report that confirmed and extended an earlier study done by the U.S. Surgeon General. As a result of these and other findings, the American Psychological Association passed a resolution in February 1985 informing broadcasters and the public of the potential dangers that viewing violence on television can have for children.

What does the research show? In the fifteen years that have passed since these events, researchers continue to study the psychological effects of seeing violence on television. Three of the major effects that have been observed are:

- Children may become less sensitive to the pain and suffering of others.
- Children may be more fearful of the world around them.
- Children may be more likely to behave in aggressive or harmful ways toward others.

Researchers are concerned that children who watch a lot of TV are more desensitized by violent scenes than children who watch only a little TV. In other words, children who watch more TV are less bothered by violence in general and less likely to see anything wrong with it. A number of studies have demonstrated that people who watch a violent program instead of a nonviolent one are slower to intervene or to call for help when, at a later point in time, they see younger children fighting or playing destructively. Studies have demonstrated that children who watch a lot of television are more likely to think that the world is a mean and dangerous place. This is true for adults too.

We have become so accustomed to violence in the media that we don't notice ordinary muggings and murders—they have to be really spectacular to get us upset. And so we are being exposed to news and entertainment programs featuring the most nightmarish of visions. As a sociologist and a mother of two teenage children, I find this deeply disturbing.
—Pepper Schwartz, Ph.D., University of Washington

In spite of the accumulated evidence, broadcasters, scientists, and politicians continue to debate the link between the viewing of TV violence and children's aggressive behavior. Some broadcasters and political leaders believe that there is not enough evidence to prove that TV violence is harmful. But scientists who have studied this issue say that there is a link between TV violence and aggression; in 1992, the American Psychological Association's Task Force on Television and Society published a report confirming this view. The report, "Big World, Small Screen: The Role of Television in American Society," concludes that the harmful effects of TV violence clearly exist.

What's Your View?

Parents differ greatly in their views about media violence in the home. Is that crazy cartoon coyote really the victim or victim-

izer of the Roadrunner? Do their animated adventures really influence a young child's attitudes about violence? Do TV shows
and films, which often show females as the targets of psycho-
pathic males, contribute to attitudes about males being victimizers and females being victims? What are the consequences of
violent acts on TV or films? How do "heroes" justify their
killing?

When you were growing up, did you have a parent who
talked with you about the TV shows and films you viewed? Did
they point out who was portrayed as victim, victimizer, or
observer? Consider the reflections of the following parents as
they look back on their childhood talks about violence in the
media.

*I think it would be great if a group of teenage boys actually could talk
about their feelings and why movie characters acted in a certain way
instead of just commenting on how cool the weapons were.*
—Tess, mother of two, Memphis, Tennessee

I don't know if Xena, the Warrior Princess *is a step forward. She
seems to kill as many people as James Bond, except she offers a line
of remorse after slicing open bad Roman soldiers.*
—Mary, mother of two, Syracuse, New York

*My mom didn't mind violent TV shows as long as they had a good story
with interesting characters. We always watched thrillers, but they
weren't the graphic movies with blood like they have today. She always said that the writer had to be smarter than the audience is. She*

was more upset by plot holes than by guns. It got me thinking at a very early age about how TV was scripted.
—Dave, father of one, Jamestown, New York

I would rather let my two girls watch movies like Scream *than movies with explicit sex scenes. I find gratuitous sex more offensive than gratuitous violence.*
—Heather, mother of two, West Linn, Oregon

Just What the Doctor Ordered

The American Academy of Pediatrics has come out in favor of parents managing their children's TV viewing. Some health professionals see the influence of the media as a public health concern. Imagine a future in which you take your child to the doctor for a checkup and you're asked for your child's medical history and media history. Consider answering the following questions from the American Academy of Pediatrics about your children's exposure to television, movies, video games, the Internet, and other media.

- Does your child watch more than one to two hours of television a day?
- Do you watch television with your child, or know what your child is watching?
- Do you discuss television shows with your child?
- Does your child have a television in his or her room?
- Do you limit your child's watching of television shows that of-

ten contain violence, sex, foul or explicit language, or images of tobacco or alcohol use?
- Does your child have nightmares or trouble sleeping after watching movies?
- Do you allow your child to own or rent videos or computer games with violent content?

How do you feel about these questions? In the real world of overworked parents, how much media can you realistically monitor?

Peer Pressure to Watch

All of us feel peer pressure to dress, act, or talk a certain way. The pressure is especially intense for school-age children—some kids say that pressure from friends and schoolmates is the single biggest influence in their daily lives. Is your child under pressure to consume violent programming? Does your child fight with his friends for control of the remote to find the grizzliest TV shows, or compete to rent the bloodiest video? Do you have a child who obsesses over a particularly violent TV show, film, or song? Does your child have peers who favor particularly violent media content or programming in which particular types of people are victims? If so, who are the victims? Are they females or people of a particular race, economic condition, religion, or lifestyle?

The power of marketing is truly amazing. And my two boys seem to be prime targets when a new action film comes out. It's the same routine. First the commercials hit the TV, then all the fast food tie-ins, and then the action toys. And then I hear, "Mom, everyone is seeing it so we have to go." —Pam, mother of two, Gaithersburg, Maryland

Giving Your Child the Big Picture

Number of hours the average American spends watching TV per day: 4

Amount of time the average American has spent watching TV by age 65: 9 years

(Source: Teenage Research Unlimited/Mediascope, 1998)

There are many ways to frame a talk about media and how they portray violence. One angle is to focus on the roles of victims, victimizers, and observers. Why does the victimizer hurt people? What is his motivation? Are there other alternatives? You and your child may argue over who is the hero and who is the victimizer. (If the hero guns down a group of bad guys, is he now a victimizer?) The child may point out lots of good reasons to kill and maim: to protect the universe, the army, the town, and the family—or just to get even. Ask your child to think about other movies or TV programs he has seen. Do they tend to do the same thing?

Children today grow up perceiving themselves as media savvy in a media-saturated world. Many can discuss what is on the screen and who works behind the camera. You can ask your child why she thinks the show was scripted the way it was. Were the actors given smart lines or did they seem dumb? Why did the director cast men in some roles and females in others? If your child had been writing the script or directing the show, what might she have done differently?

"Today's Top Story": Blood, Mayhem, and Murder

What do your local and national news programs tell your family about violence? Do they give a balanced picture of how prevalent violence is? Does their daily coverage of violent acts make you and your children feel safer or more insecure? Make sure that if your child watches the news, you treat the news as you would any TV show. Let your child know that news programs are scripted just like many TV shows, and that their focus is on grabbing your attention and getting ratings. Each news program has its own special perspective, and your child needs to know that it's not the only perspective. When a newscaster reports a violent act, ask your child what she thinks of the story and whether it was reported accurately and fairly. Children often tend to think of the news as "the truth." With the blending of entertainment and journalism, we need to view TV news programs with an even sharper critical eye than we view prime-time entertainment.

When I was growing up we only knew about what happened in our city. Now we get fifty stations telling us about every little violent event around the world. It's no wonder people become desensitized to what's happening in their own neighborhood.
—Milly, mother of four, grandmother of ten, Kansas City, Missouri

To tell the truth, it's not horror movies that give me nightmares. It's the nightly news. The world they show is a very scary place. If I be-

lieved everything I saw on the news I don't think I could leave my home.—Brandy, mother of two, Dalton, Georgia

The three most dramatic events etched into my memory are the news shows covering the murders of President Kennedy, Robert Kennedy, and Martin Luther King. I was in first grade and the world seemed to stop when the president was killed. All four stations kept showing the same images over and over again.—Sue, Seattle, Washington

Different Families: Different Values

Everyone defines acceptable levels of violence in the media in his or her own way. Here are some examples of media content that may be experienced differently depending on a person's background:

A news program repeatedly shows clips of bloodied children escaping from an actual high school shooting.

Some parents see the images of children bleeding from gunshot wounds as important elements of the news coverage, while others find the repeated showing of graphic images sensational and unnecessary. Some parents feel that this kind of programming gives the incorrect picture that all schools are "time bombs" waiting to go off.

■

A TV drama portrays an unhappy student who learns how to make a bomb off the Internet and gets ready to blow up his school.

Some view this as a typical Tuesday night of TV, while others see this as a guide to sociopathic behavior.

■

A computer game requires players to kill the enemy, collect weapons, and lose points if they wipe out innocent bystanders.

Some view this as a harmless adventure game while others see it as too intense and a poor moral lesson about how to deal with "enemies."

Last-minute Checkups before the Talk

Before you talk with your child, it helps to think back to your own childhood feelings about TV violence.

- When you were a child, were there clear rules on what kinds of violent shows you could watch?
- Did a parent talk with you about violent events in the news?
- Did you ever have bad dreams after seeing violent images in the media?
- How different is life for your child?
- Do you have clear family rules about what kinds of shows, films, or videos she can watch?
- Have you talked with him about violence in the media?
- Does she ever have bad dreams as a result of seeing violent images in the media?

This is a good time to think about your childhood experiences with violence in the media. Do you have any stories that you can share with your child? For example:

- An experience watching violence on the news and how it made you feel
- A movie you saw that changed your views on violence

Consider telling your child about the news programs, TV shows, or movies you grew up watching and how they shaped your view of the world.

What Are Your Family Rules?

Do you have family rules about what kinds of TV programs, films, and videos your child can watch? If not, this is a good time to think about them. The talk outlined in this chapter highlights the following situations:

- A family talking about a TV show
- A boy and girl watching a violent movie in which a man kills lots of women
- A family watching a news report on a school shooting

Talking about each of these situations will raise issues about violence in the media. What rules have you discussed with your child about TV, films, or computer games? Do you allow your child to have a TV in his own room? Do you ask what kinds of movies she is going to see? Do you preview electronic games he wants to buy? Do you know what videos she is renting? Do you know what ratings his music has? These are the kinds of questions that can bring up your family rules about violence in the media. At the end of the talk you will have a chance to review your family rules with your child.

The Talk

Introduce the Talk

With *Ten Talks* nearby, you could tell your child: "I'd like to get your views about TV."

A good time for this talk might be just after the TV has been turned off, or just before it's turned on. You can begin your talk by asking: "What does media mean?"

After identifying some examples such as TV shows, cable news shows, film, video, radio, billboard advertising, and the Internet, you may proceed with the next section. Note that Chapter Eight will focus on the Internet.

Review These Words

Please review the terms in this section. Discussing all the terms with your child is optional. You know what's appropriate for your child's age and maturity level. More than likely, even the youngest children have heard these words on TV.

critic: a judge of media. For example, "The movie critic said the movie was worth seeing because it had an interesting message, and was well scripted and acted."

media: TV, films, video, cable, newspapers, radio, billboards, magazines

media literacy: the ability to analyze and judge media and to see what kinds of messages are being sent and why

news: reports of recent events, in print or on the radio, TV, or the Internet. Each news show has its own perspective on the day's events

propaganda: systematic spreading of unquestioned ideas and beliefs

ratings: rankings or classification by content. For example, TV programs have ratings based on the types of violence and sexual activity they include.

Why Is Talking about Violence in the Media Important?

Let your child tell you why talking about violence in the media is important. Some responses might be:

- Some TV shows and films can teach us what to do when something violent happens.
- Some TV shows and films can show us how harmful and painful violence is and can teach us not to be violent.
- Talking about violence on TV can help us become better critics of TV, film, and news programming.
- Talking about violence in the media means clarifying family rules about ratings, TV and film viewing, music, and electronic games.

The Stories

In the next part of the talk, you'll be reading short stories to your child and discussing them together. You don't have to read all of the stories. Pick the ones that you think are appropriate for your child. The stories are very simple. Feel free to embellish them, adding details that you think might make the story more believable and inviting to your child.

The Story about TV Night

This story gives you an opportunity to discuss violence on TV.

"Dad, Mom, and their son and daughter have just finished watching a TV show about a superhero that kills bad guys. The family is talking about the TV show."

Ask these questions of your child:

- What is the dad saying?
- What is the mom saying?
- What is the son saying?
- What is the daughter saying?

Now that your child has completed this scenario, ask the following questions:

- Was there any violence on the TV show? If so, what kind?
- Were there any victims, victimizers, or observers in the show? If so, who was in what role?
- What might be entertaining about the TV show?
- Why do companies make TV shows like this?

- What were the commercials for? Why would those advertisers want to sponsor a show like this?
- How often should families talk about the TV shows they watch?
- How often should families watch TV shows together?
- What could a family talk about after a TV show?

Follow up with any questions you feel are appropriate given your child's responses.

Clarify Your Family's Values

Discuss these questions with your child as a way of sharing your values about violence in the media. A number of potential responses from children are included to help you formulate your own responses.

Ask your child: "If children watch hundreds of programs that show people using violence to solve their problems, can it have an impact on their attitudes about how to solve problems?"

Child response #1: I don't know.
Parent: We learn from role modeling. Kids learn things by watching their parents. Kids also learn things from watching TV. If kids only see people using violence to solve problems, then they might think that violence is the only way to solve problems.

Child response #2: It's only TV, not reality.
Parent: That's right. Sometimes it's simulated violence, but sometimes TV shows are about "reality," with networks like

122

CNN. Whether news or entertainment programming, the messages about violence are real. And media messages are powerful. They tell us what to think. A lot of media messages say that using violence to solve problems is not only good, it's heroic. This is not a message I'm happy with. In real life, we all need to be able to communicate our thoughts and feelings to solve our problems. I want to see messages in the media that support this point of view.

The Story about Horror Films

This gives you a chance to discuss violent programming and who the victims and victimizers are in horror films.

"A boy and girl have gone to see a movie. They are watching a movie about a man who kills lots of women. On the screen the man attacks a woman."

Ask these questions of your child:

- What is the boy thinking?
- What is the girl thinking?

Now that your child has completed this scenario, ask the following questions:

- Who is the victim in the movie?
- Who is the victimizer?
- What might the boy and girl talk about after the movie?

- How old should people be to see movies like this?
- What might be entertaining about this movie?
- Have you ever seen a movie like this? If so, how did you feel about it?
- Why do companies make movies like this?
- What are our family rules about watching movies like this?

Follow up with any questions that you feel are appropriate given your child's responses.

Clarify Your Family's Values

Discuss these questions with your child as a way of sharing your values about violence in the media.

Ask your child: "If people watch thousands of TV shows where men use violence against women, can it affect their attitudes about men and women in real life?"

Child response #1: I don't know.
Parent: We know that some men can be violent toward women. Lots of TV shows and films show men being violent toward women. The message in these kinds of shows upsets me. I don't like seeing females as victims. I don't like seeing females made to look defenseless. I don't think that it helps boys or girls to see anyone, male or female, tortured or killed.

Child response #2: There are TV shows with women who kill, too.
Parent: I don't want to see women acting violent any more than

I want to see men acting violent. It's good to see strong women who are not victims, but I'd rather they be both strong and respectful of human life.

The Story about the News

This story gives you an opportunity to discuss what your child sees on the news.

"A boy and girl are watching a cartoon when there is a commercial for the news. The story is about a boy who has shot and killed some students at his school."

Ask these questions of your child:

- What is the boy saying?
- What is the girl saying?
- What is the boy thinking?
- What is the girl thinking?

Now that your child has completed this scenario, ask the following questions:

- Why do news programs spotlight violence in schools?
- What kind of information about violence and safety would you want to get from the news?
- Who writes the news? Who decides what stories go into a news show?

- Have you ever seen news programs about a school shooting?
- If so, how did you feel?

Follow up with any questions that you feel are appropriate given your child's responses.

Clarify Your Family's Values

Ask this question of your child as a way of sharing your values about violence in the media.

Parent: If children watch hundreds of news programs that show people being violent, can it affect their attitudes about violence in real life? Is the world as violent a place as the news tells us?

Child: I don't know.

Parent: There are some parts of the world that are very violent places. There are parts of the United States that are violent, too. Even though there is the rare school shooting, statistics show that schools are some of the safest places to be. Of course, even one shooting at a school is one too many. The news makes it sound very different. The news about violence can make people afraid and distrustful of others. The news rarely, if ever, starts with headlines about the good things happening in the world and problems being solved. News programs are like other commercial entertainment in that they also need good ratings.

The Bare Minimum: A Quick Quiz for Kids

Ask your child the following questions to assess her knowledge of violence in the media.

1. Can you give me one reason why so many companies make movies and TV that are violent?
   Sample answers:
   • For TV—to get good ratings, which lets them charge more for advertising.
   • For films—to attract lots of young male viewers, considered a good market by movie companies.

2. Why do news programs like to use stories that contain violence?
   Sample answer:
   • To attract viewers, which means better ratings, which means more advertising dollars.

3. Why do people like to watch violent movies or TV shows?
   Sample answer:
   • It's an escape from reality.

4. What is your favorite action movie? Who are the victims, victimizers, observers, and heroes?

5. What is your favorite action TV show? Who are the victims, victimizers, observers, and heroes?

6. Name a TV show or movie that you didn't like because of its violent content or unrealistic characters.

Talk about Your Family Rules

This is an opportunity to review your family rules. Ask your child the following question:

What are our family rules about watching violence in the media?
Sample answers:

- TV viewing is limited to two hours on a school night.
- Video and film titles are approved by a parent before renting or viewing.
- Electronic games that show excessive violence are not appropriate for young people. I'd like to review your ideas for purchases to see how much glorified violence they contain.
- Publications that glorify violence are not welcome in this house.

After the Talk

After the talk about violence in the media, many parents report learning more about their child's viewing habits. Some parents were surprised to hear about their children viewing adult movies at their friends' homes. Others found that even the smallest child had acquired a taste for very violent films.

A Moment to Reflect

Take a moment to reflect on the talk you just had with your child.

- Do you feel comfortable with your child's ability to analyze media content?
- Were you concerned about his views on the news about school shootings?
- Are you comfortable enforcing the rules about TV viewing?

- How much of the time were you listening to your child?
- Did you feel that you needed to read between the lines of his comments?

Warning Signs

The talks also may reveal potential problems your child might have. There may be cause for concern if you see that your child

- would spend most of his day watching violent programs on TV if you let him.
- finds extreme violence in films and TV shows funny.
- is modeling his behavior after violent characters.

As with all the talks, use your intuition. If your child seems obsessed with violent media content to the point where he is neglecting his schoolwork and household chores, you may consider getting help from a counselor.

Finding Help

If this talk revealed what you consider to be a serious problem—for example, compulsive watching of violent TV shows or a near addiction to electronic games—there may be cause for concern. People of all ages use TV as an escape, and your child's behavior may be perfectly normal for his age. But if you still feel unsettled by something you heard, consider talking with a trained counselor or a therapist, or checking in with your child's teacher on your child's behavior and academic progress.

Success Stories

Talk number four is done. Good work! If you're like most parents, you've gotten some surprises during this talk. Lots of parents report hearing that their kids were watching questionable programs at friends' houses—or even at home when no one else was around. Remember that getting new information, even the unsettling kind, is a huge success in itself. As a result of this talk, one mom in Gaithersburg, Maryland, now reviews every video game her son wants to purchase. A mom in Syracuse, New York, said she had one of the most interesting conversations she's ever had with her daughter—about *Xena, Warrior Princess!* The parent wasn't necessarily happy with everything she heard, but that she heard it at all qualifies as a major success.

Sample Talks

Between Parents and Children

If you are wondering how a talk based on this chapter might really sound, take a look at the following excerpts from real family talks.

Discussing the Story about TV Night

Participants: a mother and her fourth-grade son.

Mom: This is a story about TV night. A dad and mom and their son and daughter have just finished watching a TV show. The

TV show is about a superhero that kills bad guys. The family is talking about the TV show. What is the dad saying about the TV show?

Child: Wait. Is this show gory? Or like *Batman* or like *Dragonball Z* . . . or what?

Mom: Which one do you want it to be like?

Child: Um . . . *Dragonball Z* (Note: This is an animated Japanese cartoon that the mother and child had talked about earlier in the day. After watching the show together, the mother said she didn't want her son to watch it because it showed so much fighting and violence without it adding to the story. The son argued it was no more violent than any other, for example, *Superman*.)

Mom: Okay, it's like *Dragonball Z*. What does the mom think of that?

Child: She thinks, "Wow, it's pretty violent."

Mom: What is the son saying?

Child: "Whoa, this is cool."

Mom: And what is the daughter saying?

Child: "This is stupid."

Mom: Okay. Was there any violence in the TV show? If so, what kind?

Child: Yes . . . but not really.

Mom: Were there any victims, victimizers, or observers in the show?

Child: There was everything.

Mom: Why do companies make TV shows like this?

Child: Because they are exciting.

Mom: What do the companies who make the shows want you to buy?

Child: Oh, are you talking about the commercials?

Mom: Yes.

Child: They were advertising one thing . . . this Hot-Rocker thing.

Mom: Is that a toy?

Child: Yes, it's like a motorcycle.

Mom: How often do families talk about the TV shows they watch?

Child: Not too often, since they usually watch different things.

Lessons Learned from This Sample Talk

The parent listened to her son talk about programming he likes. In previous talks he had argued that a program he wasn't allowed to watch was no more violent than programs he can watch now. The parent might ask: How do you feel when you see people maimed or killed in action TV programs? How do you feel when you see people maimed or killed on news programs? Future talks provide an opportunity for parent and child to discuss what pull the advertisers have on him as well as what kinds of programs exist that might be of interest to the entire family.

Discussing the Story about Horror Films

Participants: a divorced father and his sixth-grade daughter.

Dad: A boy and girl are watching a movie about a man who kills lots of women. On the screen the man attacks a woman. What is the boy thinking, watching this movie? You know about this because you watch these kinds of movies with your mother. I don't have that kind of movie here in this house.

Daughter: I think it all depends on the type of boy. For instance, if it was a really bad boy, I think he would be saying, like, "GO KILL HER!" and he'd be waiting for the next killing.

Dad: Would he be rooting for the violence?

Daughter: He would say, "Come on, let's kill another girl. Let's GO, GO." And would be really into it. I think.

Dad: What do you think the girl is thinking about as she watches that man killing women?

Daughter: I think that the girl would be really scared about it.

Dad: Young girls are more vulnerable because guys are stronger than girls. That's why girls are easier to make a victim of violence than boys, because girls aren't as strong as guys. Who is the victim in the movie scene?

Daughter: The woman is the victim.

Dad: Who is the victimizer? That's the person who goes after the victim.

Daughter: The killer, the man.

Dad: What might the boy and girl talk about after the movie?

Daughter: The boy would probably say, "WOW! THAT WAS SOOOO COOOL! DID YOU SEE THAT, DID YOU SEE THE BLOOOD!" But the girl will probably keep her fright inside of her. She'll be cool and think, "Okay, this may happen to me but I just have to get ready and prepare."

Dad: How old should people be to see movies like that?

Daughter: I think that you should be, maybe, about to turn thirteen through eighteen or nineteen. It's up to the parent.

Dad: But the movies are rated, so the parent needs to look at the movie rating first before they take their child to see it. And so, do you think it should be the decision of the parent or the child whether the child sees the movie?

Daughter: I think it's more the parent, because the parent is the adult.

Dad: Why do film companies make horror movies? What are they trying to promote to the public?

Daughter: I don't really know.

Dad: Do you think some people like scary stuff? Do some people like to be scared and be squirming in their seats, even though they know it's all make-believe?

Daughter: Yeah. I think that the filmmakers are adults, and they want to make them to scare people, like that intense feeling.

Dad: Do you think they make them for children or for adults?

Daughter: I think they make them mostly for teenagers and adults. I don't think they make them for children.

Dad: What are our family rules about watching movies like this?

Daughter: Well . . .

Dad: What are *my* rules in *this* household?

Daughter: *Your* rules are that we cannot watch scary movies.

Dad: What did I do with all our scary movies?

Daughter: You gave all our scary movies to Mom because you didn't want us to watch them.

Dad: All right. To summarize this, how do you feel about scary movies, and do you like to watch them?

Daughter: Right now, I'm in the sixth grade and I hate getting scared. I hardly watch any scary movies.

Dad: Some people are not really affected by it. They know it's just a movie.

Daughter: Well I get affected by it a lot because I have an imagination, and I think that they're alive and they're out there and come out at night on Halloween.

Lessons Learned from This Sample Talk

Although the child's mother and father have different households and family rules about watching violent movies, the talk allowed the father and daughter to clarify why young children should not watch this type of movie. This situation highlights the importance of both parents being aware of each other's household rules and attitudes. The daughter's statement, "Okay, this may happen to me but I just have to get ready and prepare," is important to follow up on. The parent might ask: Do you feel that you need to prepare for violence? How do you feel, thinking about movies where there are murders? How safe do you feel after you watch a scary movie? Do you ever feel pressure from family members or friends to watch scary movies? If so, what can I do to help?

Discussing the Story about Horror Films

Participants: a mother and her eighth-grade son.

Mom: A boy and girl are watching a movie about a man who kills lots of women. On the screen the man attacks a woman. What is the boy thinking?

Child: I don't know.

Mom: Have you ever watched a slasher movie?

Child: You never let me. I wanted to watch *Scream,* but noooo.

Mom: What would you be thinking if I ever let you watch one of those movies?

Child: (long pause as he mumbles)

Mom: Okay, what is the girl thinking?

Child: I'm not a girl, I don't know.

Mom: Okay, well, let's just pretend. So they are watching this movie and it's about a man and he's killing all these women, like in *The Boston Strangler.* Who is the victim in this scene?

Child: What do you think? The women.

Mom: Who is the victimizer?

Child: Duh, the man.

Mom: What might the boy and girl talk about after seeing a movie like this?

Child: Good movie . . . bad movie. I don't know.

Mom: Okay, how about a movie like *Scream.* What did people say about that movie?

Child: It was pretty cool.

Mom: Why?

Child: 'Cause it was.

Mom: Do you know why?

Child: No.

Mom: Do you think they might be too frightening?

Child: No.

Mom: Do you think they depict people in the way that they should be depicted?

Child: I don't know what you're talking about.

Mom: Do these movies show people who have a grudge against society, and who decide to go out and kill a lot of people? Do the movies make them look like anti-heroes? Do you know what an anti-hero is?

Child: Someone who fights against a hero?

Mom: It's someone who is like Norman, the star of *Psycho.* You saw how they made you feel sorry for Norman Bates?

Child: Yes.

Mom: Well, that's what I'm talking about. They make you feel sorry for Norman, who is the star of the movie and who's going around killing people. That's a disturbing thing to see.

Lessons Learned from This Sample Talk

This talk illustrates what happens when a child is very resistant to talking about violence in media. This son was angry with his mom for censoring *Scream.* It might be interesting for the child to hear about the parent's criteria for screening movies. Why was *Scream* denied but the equally violent *Psycho* allowed? Is the child getting mixed messages about what is acceptable to his mom? Even though this mom later described this talk as similar to "pulling teeth," she was able to transmit some important concepts about anti-heroes and how she finds the use of anti-heroes in films disturbing. The parent might ask: What is the scariest movie you have ever seen? How did it make you feel? Did the movie seem real? The parent might also discuss being scared by movies as a child.

Discussing the Story about the News

Participants: a mother and her fifth-grade son.

Mom: A boy and a girl are watching a cartoon show when there is a commercial for the news. The news story is about a student who has shot some students at his school. What is the boy thinking?

Child: "Whoa."

Mom: What is the girl thinking?

Child: She is quiet and glued to the TV.

Mom: Are they upset?

Child: Yeah, I guess.

Mom: Why do news programs spotlight violence in schools? Why do they show it a lot?

Child: They show it to you to show you what happened so you won't do it.

Mom: Who writes the news? Who decides what stories go into the news?

Child: The news people, the interviewers. The directors.

Mom: Has anything like this ever happened to you or to a friend? Like you are watching TV and then the commercial for the news says, "Coming up in the news," and they highlight something that's violent.

Child: Yeah.

Mom: You remember what the news program was about?

Child: It was about Columbine.

Lessons Learned from This Sample Talk

This mom is pointing out that the news may not always portray the simple facts. Rather, news, like other TV programming, may sensationalize a violent act. This talk can be expanded to further explore the impact of news about school violence on her child. The parent might ask: How did you feel when you saw the news programs about the shootings at Columbine High School? How do you feel when you talk about Columbine today? What other news programs have made you feel scared or upset?

5

Running the Obstacle Course

Talking about School Safety

When I was a kid I knew I would be safe once I got into a classroom with the teacher. But getting to and from school, and surviving lunch and breaks were not easy. I was small, on my own, and at the mercy of the bigger guys.—Dan, father of two, San Antonio, Texas

There is no "trend" toward shootings at schools. In fact, such attacks have been on the decline. . . . The good news is that schools are some of the safest places in America.—Vincent Schiraldi, Justice Policy Institute, Washington Post, Aug. 25, 1998

I was walking through the doors of an elementary school, on my way to teach a parent workshop, and passed a giant poster saying "Gun Free Zone." Suddenly I felt like things were not okay.
—Susan Burgess, therapist, Seattle, Washington

How safe are the more than 52 million students in the elementary, middle, and high schools of the United States? School shootings make the headlines and shatter our image of school as a safe haven for youth. Thankfully, school shootings are not commonplace. But that does not mean there is no cause for concern.

What doesn't make the headlines are the everyday forms of physical aggression and threats of violence including verbal abuse, harassment, coercion, intimidation, and physical assault. Starting in elementary school and continuing through high school, violence demeans, intimidates, and frightens children.

Schools are designed to educate our children, and they also are supposed to teach them to get along, respect one another, play fair, and follow the rules. But teachers can't watch every student every minute. In those unsupervised times—before school starts, during lunch, in the hallways, on the bus—students find ways to issue subtle and overt threats, dictate a pecking order, establish groups and gangs, and commit violence against one another. All of this may sound very familiar to you because school was once a place where you spent a lot of time. You now have the chance to help your child better understand the social challenges and opportunities school life presents. You can't prevent every hallway harassment from happening to her, but you can prepare her for what's ahead as she moves from grade to grade.

Preparing for the Talk

In the school environment, your child may take on different roles, including the victim, victimizer, or observer. The vast majority of students are observers, whether passive or active, of threats and violence during school. In this talk you will let your child know that

- she has the right to a school environment that is safe from violence and intimidation.

- she should be able to report violence or threats of violence without fear of reprisal.
- there are ways she can express her anger and frustration at school without resorting to violent behavior.

What You Can Expect from This Talk

After the talk your child will

- be able to identify school policies and rules which are meant to protect students from violence.
- understand the importance of respecting other people at school and to expect respect from others.
- know where to go for help if problems about violence at school arise.
- know the family rules about violent behavior and safety at school.

About Violence and School Safety

All teachers want a safe school environment, and guidelines exist to help every school administrator develop and enforce safety rules, provide conflict resolution programs, and offer parent involvement programs. Each school develops its own standard of safety. It's an ongoing process that requires the help of state and local government as well as committed educators and informed parents. You, however, are best equipped to help your child deal with the problems they will face at school.

The images of children being shot at school are horrifying. But the news frenzy to profile the victims and victimizers and to point blame does little to calm the fears and anxieties of school children, parents, and teachers. Your child should be assured that school shootings are very rare. As you read the following statistics, keep in mind that there are approximately 52 million students in grades K–12:

Number of school shooting deaths in 1992–93: 55

Number of school shooting deaths in 1997–98: 40
> *(Source: National School Safety Center at Pepperdine University)*

Proportion of U.S. public schools reporting one or more violent crimes in 1996–97: 10%
> *(Source: Violence and Discipline Problems in U.S. Public Schools: 1996–97, National Center for Education Statistics)*

Percentage of American teenagers who think their school could be struck by the kind of massacre that devastated Columbine High School in Littleton, Colorado: 52%
> *(Source: New York Times/CBS News poll, Oct. 1999)*

How do you interpret the statistics above? The data indicate that violence at school is on the decline. Schools are safer than homes and neighborhood streets. However, the data can't capture the daily intimidation and threats, and the fear students feel. Much of the threatening behavior at school will never be recorded—and may not even be seen as violence by the people compiling the numbers. Think back to your experience in school. How much of the unspoken intimidation you saw or felt would have been captured by statistics?

When I was teaching I was amazed at the amount of intolerance and name-calling that went on, much of it having to do with race. Students would come up to me, visibly shaken, saying, "He called me a blank"—fill in the racial slur. Zero tolerance for harassment of any kind is a goal. We don't accept it in the workplace, and there is no place for it in the school.

—Frieda Takamura, Washington Education Association

What Are the Rules at Your Child's School?

Each school has its own policies and rules about what is permissible, acceptable, and enforceable. This would be a good time to review your child's school's policies regarding safety and violence. To obtain a copy of your child's school safety guidelines, call the school office. Some schools have a variety of regulations addressing everything from weapons to sexual harassment. Others have rules but no stated policy or procedures for enforcement. Some have committed to training all school personnel on safety as well as offering parent workshops. Education leaders understand the complexity of the problem. Consider the following excerpt from *The School Safety Manual*, developed by the National Education Association:

As places where children congregate for up to six hours a day, schools are where violence occurs when the problems children face in the community or in their families are not resolved in those places. For school safety plans to succeed . . . they must include school personnel as leaders and the following as members: community activists, religious leaders, businesspeople, and representatives of governmental agencies, protective and health services, and other groups concerned with school violence.

Community safety plans must include community representatives as leaders and parents and school personnel as members.

Parent anti-violence plans must include parents as leaders and community representatives and school personnel as advisers.

Parents are a vital component in any school-based strategy to keep schools safe. It is important that school personnel, community members, and parents recognize that they must all be involved in keeping schools safe. Consider bringing your expertise and insight to your child's school safety program.

Pressure from Your Child's Peers

How safe does your child feel at school? When you ask your child, you may find that pushing, shoving, touching, name-calling, and unwanted fondling is very common. Even with laws and policies in place to promote more respectful behavior, intimidation and threats are still part of the school experience for many students.

It's likely that most students don't see getting help as an option. From the student's point of view, reporting a classmate to school administrators would mean being singled out as a "loser"—someone who can't handle his or her own problems. This problem is similar to that of girls who report sexual harassment. Students may not be believed, and in some cases the intimidation experienced by the "reporter" becomes worse than the actual experience of being harassed. For a child trying to make it through school, the risks of reporting violence may not seem worth it.

Part of your talk about violence in school is to find out how your child is dealing with his day-to-day school life and what he does to feel safe. Is your child joining teams or student clubs or gangs to create a sense of security at school? Does she have a strong network of school friends to support her? The talk in this chapter can give you insight into your child's ability to find support from peers at school. You also may get a sense of the kinds of people your child is spending time with and the values they have.

Giving Your Child the Big Picture

Your child has thirteen years of elementary and secondary school, with each year growing progressively more complex academically and socially. No matter what grade your child is in, she can be assured that the next one will provide more challenges. It's her job, as your child, to do her best in each grade. It's your job, as the parent, to help your child deal with her school environment and student interactions.

Each year will offer new challenges to your child for getting along, resolving conflict, and fitting in with other students. The following questions concern some aspects of school life that you may want to discuss with your child.

1. There will be times at school when the teacher is not around and your child is on her own. How does your child cope during these unsupervised times?
2. Having friends at school makes one feel safer. What do you know about your child's social network at school? Participating in any form of extracurricular activities helps to build a social network.

3. Big students may pick on smaller students. Is your child being picked on, bullied, or threatened by anyone at school?

4. Your child may worry that if she reports being bullied or threatened, the person she told on might try to get revenge later. What's the "code of silence" in your child's school? If your child were being threatened at school, would she ever reveal it to you or a teacher?

5. Some school sports can send mixed messages to students. Sports can offer valuable lessons about teamwork, self-discipline, and fitness. At the same time, some sports can be seen as violent activities. The behaviors applauded during sports are not appropriate in the hallways between students. Does your child understand the difference between these two worlds?

6. There are many adults who work at school who can help your child. What school staff members does your child know and trust?

7. There may be an adult in or near the school environment who frightens your child. Are there any such people in your child's school environment? Has she mentioned anything about being bothered by an adult on or near the school site?

Are there other concerns you have about your school and your child's safety? You will have opportunities to share these during your talk.

Mary was a big bully in my school. When we were in line after lunch she would walk up and down the line and say things to certain kids, like "You're ugly" or "I'm going to get you." I would dread these times when I was in junior high, always fearing that she would single me

out. I look back and think about why I took such abuse. When you're little a bully looms very large.
—Suzanne, mother of three, Denver, Colorado

We have more than thirty official languages used by our children in the school district. There is a lot of diversity that can lead to a lot of acting out and name-calling. Our district did two things that seemed to be a good start. Each school developed their own harassment prevention policy and we started offering parent workshops to improve family communication.
—Judith, middle school teacher, Seattle, Washington

I tell my kids that they don't have to like their fellow students, they just have to be respectful. That's how the real world works when you get a job.—Mario, father of two, Boise, Idaho

Different Families: Different Values

Everyone defines acceptable school student behavior in his or her own way. Here are some behaviors that may be experienced differently depending on a person's background:

A boy lifts a girl's skirt at lunch.

Some parents call this sexual harassment, while others call it intimidation. Some would dismiss it as flirting, a practical joke, or playing.

■

A bigger student tells a smaller student he doesn't like his face and is going to beat him up after school.

Some parents call this intimidation and a threat of violence, while others call it "boys being boys" and perfectly normal behavior.

■

A popular girl taunts a shy boy at school, calling him names that ridicule him.

Some parents say that boys can take care of themselves around girls and don't need help from adults. Others would say that this is harassment, noting that females are just as capable of harassing a male as males are of harassing females.

Last-minute Checkups before the Talk

Before you talk to your child, it helps to think back to how you felt about violence at school when you were young.

• Did you feel safe going to and from school?
• How safe did you feel during lunch or recess?
• Did you worry about violence or threats in the locker room?
• Would you have felt safe reporting harassment to a teacher?

Think about your child in school today.

• Does she feel safe going to and from school?
• Have you asked her how she feels during lunch, recess, and other unsupervised times?
• Would he feel comfortable reporting threats or harassment to you or to a teacher?

149

- How much time does your child spend worrying about threats or violence at school?

This is a good time to think about your first experiences with violence and harassment as a child. Do you have any stories that you can share with your child? For example:

- A peer who called you names or threatened you
- An experience confronting a bully
- How teachers handled troublemakers
- What happened when someone reported on another student for bullying

At some point in your talk, some of these experiences might be helpful to discuss with your child.

What Are Your Family Rules?

Do you have family rules about school safety? If not, this is a good time to think about them. The talk outlined in this chapter highlights the following situations:

- A boy pushing another boy
- A group of boys threatening a boy
- A group of girls threatening a girl

Addressing these situations will give you an opportunity to discuss your family rules. What would you want your child to do in each situation? What are your expectations? Before the talk, think about what rules you want to communicate with your child. At the end of the talk, you will have the chance to review the rules with your child.

The Talk

Introduce the Talk

Find a time for an uninterrupted ten minutes or more. With this book in hand, tell your child: "I'd like to talk with you about school and how safe you feel there."

She may be relieved to hear that you are not going to talk with her about her grades.

You could say, "What are some examples of violence at school?"

She may offer some examples, such as shooting, stabbing, beating, pushing, shoving, name-calling, or threats from older students. If so, proceed with the next section.

If she doesn't offer examples of school violence, say something like, "Examples of school violence might be someone pushing you, calling you names, threatening or intimidating you, or demanding lunch money from you."

Review These Words

Please review the terms in this section. Discussing all the terms with your child is optional. You may want to review these words and definitions with your child. You know what's appropriate for your child's age and maturity level. More than likely, even the youngest children have heard these words on TV.

bully: slang for victimizer, aggressor, a person who intimidates others

conflict resolution: courses or classes that give people the skills to mediate conflicts between people, such as the ability to break up a fight or stop a fight before it begins

counselor: a school staff person who provides help to students

harassment: repeatedly bothering, annoying, or threatening another person

intimidation: controlling someone through fear or threats

peer pressure: the psychological pressure a person feels to fit in with others, to follow the group

school safety: guidelines for keeping the school a safe and violence-free place

sexual harassment: behavior such as name-calling or touching of a sexual nature that interferes with a student's ability to learn at school

verbal abuse: name-calling, often a form of sexual harassment or intimidation

violence prevention guidelines: part of a school safety program that provides strategies for students and their parents and education staff to make school safe from violence

Why Is Talking about School Safety Important?

Students often challenge their teachers with the question, "Why do we have to learn this?" Likewise, your child may ask, "Why do we have to talk about violence at school?"

Some responses might be:

• I know that sometimes there can be problems with fellow students at school.

- I hear about problems with violence at some schools from the news and want to know more about your school—and hear it directly from you.
- I want to know how I can help.
- That's part of my job as a parent.
- I care about you.
- I care about your safety.
- I want to know what kind of support you have at school—from students or staff.

My son had a problem in 6th grade with a small group of boys who would hit other boys on the shoulder to see what kind of reaction they might get. My son told them to get lost, but his friend Neil, half his size, hit one kid back. Neil got punched for half the school year, but he liked the attention and couldn't wait to show how tough he was.
—Vanessa, mother of three, Boise, Idaho

I asked my daughter what kind of violence she has seen at school. She said the only violence she has seen is between her friend Sharon and Sharon's boyfriend Rick. She says they are always yelling at each other. I asked my daughter what she thought of their relationship. She said, "If a boy ever treated me that way, I'd dump him on the spot."
—Sue, mother of two, Portland, Oregon

The Stories

In the next part of the talk, you'll be reading short stories to your child and discussing them together. You don't have to read all of the stories. Pick the ones that you think are appropriate for your child. The stories are very simple. Feel free to embellish them, adding details that you think might make the story more believable to your child.

The Story about Pushing

This gives you a chance to discuss your child's attitudes about children being pushed around.

"A small boy is standing in line waiting to get a drink of water. An older boy pushes the small boy out of line and onto the ground."

Ask these questions of your child:

- What does the older boy say?
- What does the smaller boy say?
- What is the smaller boy thinking when this happens?
- What is the older boy thinking when he is pushing the smaller boy?
- What might others in line be thinking?

Now that your child has completed this scenario, ask the following questions:

- Why would the older boy push someone?
- What would make him stop?
- Is the smaller boy being respected?
- If the smaller boy doesn't like being pushed, what should he do?

- If the smaller boy told a teacher about being pushed, what might happen to the older boy?
- If the older boy got in trouble, what might happen to the smaller boy?
- Has anything like this ever happened at school?
- If so, how did you feel? What did you do?

Follow up with any questions that you feel are appropriate given your child's responses.

The Story about Threatening a Boy

This story gives you an opportunity to discuss intimidation, being provoked, and ways to cope.

"A new student is in the cafeteria when he is approached by a group of guys. One of them, a larger boy, says, 'You made fun of me in class.' The new boy is confused. He doesn't know what the larger boy is talking about. The group of guys look like they are going to hurt the new student."

Ask these questions of your child:

- What is the new student saying?
- What is the new student thinking?
- What is the larger boy thinking?
- What are the other students thinking?

155

Now that your child has completed this scenario, ask the following questions:

- What could happen to the new student?
- Why would the larger guy want to hurt the new student?
- How can the new student escape from being hurt?
- If the new student is hurt, what can he do?
- If the new student tells a teacher about being hurt, what might happen to the larger student?
- If the larger student gets in trouble, what might happen to the new student?
- What could the observers do to stop the fight?
- Has anything like this ever happened at school? If so, what happened? How did you feel?

Follow up with any questions that you feel are appropriate given your child's responses.

The Story about Threatening a Girl

This story focuses on intimidation, being provoked, and ways to cope.

"A shy girl is waiting for the school bus to go home when she is approached by a group of girls. One of them, an older girl, says, 'You were talking with my boyfriend.' The shy girl is confused. She doesn't know what the older girl is talking about. The group of girls look like they are going to hurt the shy student."

Ask these questions of your child:

- What is the shy girl saying?
- What is the shy girl thinking?
- What is the older girl thinking?
- What are the other students thinking?

Now that your child has completed this scenario, ask the following questions:

- What could happen to the shy girl?
- Why would the older girl want to hurt the new student?
- How can the shy girl escape from being hurt?
- If the shy girl tells a teacher about being hurt, what might happen to the older girl?
- If the older girl gets in trouble, what might happen to the shy student?
- What could the observers do to prevent a fight?
- Has anything like this ever happened at school? If so, what happened? How did you feel?

Follow up with any questions that you feel are appropriate given your child's responses.

Clarify Your Family's Values

Discuss these questions with your child as a way of sharing your values about school behavior. We have included a number of potential responses from children to help you formulate your own ideas. The goal is to probe, question, explore, and engage in a dialogue. Rather than lecture, this talk can also give you insights into what role your child may be playing at school—victim, victimizer, or observer.

Parent: When a person is attacked or threatened at school, what can he or she do?

Child: Nothing.

Parent: There are things one can do. There are school rules about this, right?

Child: If you tell on someone you get in worse trouble.

Parent: If you think that reporting problems to someone at school gets you in bigger trouble with students, then I want you to tell me about it. I need to know what is happening to you. If I don't know how you are being treated, then I can't help you. I understand that reporting on a student can be risky. I remember what it was like when I was in school. I promise not to go running to your teacher or principal when you experience a threat. You and I can talk about the incident and together we can make a plan to deal with the problem. I would still like you to ask your teacher about how students can report violence, threats of violence, or harassment. What's the official procedure for reporting? You can also ask your teacher or office staff about conflict resolution classes.

■

Parent: What are our family rules about school violence?

Child: I don't know.

Parent: The family rule is that when we see violence or threats of violence we want it to stop. I want it reported to the teacher or principal. But if you think that may put you in trouble with other students, then I'd like you to report it to me. And then you and I can decide together how we want to handle it.

Parent: How can you defend yourself at school?

Child: Fight back.

Parent: Yes, but there are consequences if a person fights back. One, the fighting might get worse and people might get hurt very badly. Second, the fighting might expand and include more people. Third, everyone involved might get in trouble with the school (including the victim).

Child: Can I use self-defense?

Parent: Our family rule is to avoid hurting others and participating in violent behavior. You should try to get away from a violent person if possible. However, if necessary, I want you to defend yourself and not get hurt.

(Note: Self-defense sometimes raises more problems than it solves. Does self-defense mean permission to hit back? Often this escalates to more violent behavior. This is something you must decide, based on your beliefs.)

Parent: What happens if you report on a bully at school?

Child: Nothing.

Parent: The teacher should talk to the bully or send the bully to the principal.

Child: Maybe.

Parent: If you report on the bully, a number of things can happen. One, the bully may get punished by the school, and then get help to change his behavior. Two, if the bully knows who reported him, he may go looking for revenge. If this is you, then we need to make sure that doesn't happen by talking with the teacher, principal, and the bully's parents.

Parent: When you face problems at school with other students, how much should I try to help you and how much should you try to solve the problem yourself?

Child: I can take care of myself.

Parent: I believe that it's good for people to handle their own problems, but it's also good to know when to ask for help and this is true for kids and adults. I hope you will ask me for help when you need it.

The Story about Threats in the Hallway

This story gives you an opportunity to talk about aggressive male behavior and the potential threats of sexual coercion. (Note: younger children may not read anything sexual or suggestive into the boy's comment.)

"A girl is walking down the school hall. She sees an older student. She's only met him a few times. He looks mad. The boy looks at her and says, 'After school I want to see you—alone.' He walks off without stopping. The girl doesn't know why he said that or what it means."

Ask these questions of your child:

- What is the girl thinking?
- What is the boy thinking?

160

Now that your child has completed this scenario, ask the following questions:

- What should the girl do?
- What might she be feeling?
- Why would the boy say something like that?
- What might he be feeling?
- What happens if she reports the boy to a teacher?
- If the boy gets in trouble, what might happen to the girl?
- Has anything like this ever happened at school? If so, how did you feel? What did you do?

Follow up with any questions that you feel are appropriate given your child's responses.

Clarify Your Family's Values

The situation above focuses on intimidation and has potential sexual harassment implications. Ask the following question of your child as a way of sharing your values about school safety. We have included a number of potential responses from children to help you formulate your own responses.

Parent: When a girl feels threatened by a boy but isn't sure if it is serious or if he is teasing, what can she do?

Child: Boys are just like that.

Parent: Teasing between boys and girls can be misunderstood. Often joking between two people is fine, but if a person feels threatened, then there is a problem. Our house rule is that when you feel threatened by anything anyone says, I want to hear about it. You and I can talk about it and decide what to do. If you are the one making the jokes or threatening others, even if you don't mean it, it's not acceptable.

(Note: If you feel it is appropriate, this may be a good time to discuss sexual harassment. Legally, when anyone makes jokes of a sexual nature or makes sexual threats that interfere with either schoolwork or work, it's called sexual harassment. It is not acceptable behavior.)

The Bare Minimum: A Quick Quiz for Kids
Ask your child the following questions to assess her knowledge of violence prevention at school.

1. What are the school rules about violent behavior?
   Sample answers:
- No hitting, no disrespectful behavior, no weapons, no clothing with gang-related images, no sexual harassment

2. What happens when a student reports violence or threats to a teacher?
   Sample answers:
- The teacher and the student reporting the problem discuss it in detail.
- Sometimes the person who is accused of breaking rules is called in to explain his perspective. A school counselor or principal may become involved if the situation is serious.
- Students' parents should be notified.

Talk about Your Family Rules

What are our family rules about violent behavior at school or reporting violence or any threats at school?
Sample answers:

- If you are not sure if a threat is a joke or serious, you should still tell me about it.
- If you feel unsafe in any way at school, you should tell me about it. I can't help if I don't know about it.
- If anyone at school makes you feel unsafe, you should tell me about it.
- I will not immediately go rushing to tell your teachers everything you tell me. I promise to sit with you first and go over all the options and consequences of contacting anyone at your school.
- If for some reason you feel like you can't tell me about threats at school, then you must tell the other adults we have agreed upon.

After the Talk

After the talk with their child, many parents report that they are surprised at how much physical aggression, teasing, and threats take place at school. Your child may sound like he is getting through school with no problems, but that doesn't mean he has the ability to navigate through the school environment without incident. Young people may learn very early on that when it comes to dealing with the bullies, you just have to "take it." Your goal is to help your child understand that he has the right to a safe school. School policy, teachers, and the law are all on her side.

A Moment to Reflect

Take a moment to reflect on the talk you just had with your child. How do you feel about it?

- How has this talk changed your perception of your child's school? What surprised you about your child's school life and network of school friends?
- How do you feel about your ability to talk with your child about violence at school?
- How do you think your child felt about the talk?
- How much of the time were you listening to your child?
- What will you do differently in the next talk?

Warning Signs

The talk may reveal potential problems your child is facing, whether in the role of the victim or the victimizer. There may be cause for concern if you hear from your child that she

- is being bullied by other students.
- is afraid of another student.
- is submissive to another student.
- sees nothing wrong with bullying others.

If any of these situations come up during your talk, you may want to find out if your child's statements are indications of actual problems at school. If, after your discussion, you feel your child needs more help than you alone can offer, go see a school counselor or teacher for some assistance. If you don't receive the help you need, continue talking with the school principal. Consider putting your concerns in writing.

Finding Help

It is important for your child and all children to know that they can get help when they need it. Most districts have policies banning violence or harassment at school, although the enforcement of those policies varies from school to school. Your child's teacher, principal, school counselors, and social workers are there to help.

Success Stories

You have made it through talk number five. Congratulations! Many parents have heard about incidents at school that sound all too familiar: The schoolyard bully is alive and well. But there's always good news, too. One child in San Antonio, Texas, showed his mother the violence-prevention guidelines he and classmates had just received at school. A girl in Dalton, Georgia, told her mom about the conflict-resolution class she'd started that semester. Whatever you heard, remember that you've opened up the lines of communication about school life with your child, and that's the biggest success of all.

Sample Talks

Between Parents and Children

If you are wondering how a talk based on this chapter might really sound, take a look at the following excerpts from real family talks.

Discussing the Story about Pushing

Participants: a mother and her fourth grade daughter.

Mom: A boy is standing in line waiting for a drink of water. A bigger boy shoves the smaller boy out of the line and onto the ground. What is the smaller boy thinking when this happens?

Child: The boy is probably thinking, "Why are you doing this?"

Mom: Why is the bigger boy shoving him?

Child: He wants to get a drink and is going to fight for it. Maybe.

Mom: What do you think the smaller boy would say?

Child: "Why would you do that? What's the problem?"

Mom: What does the bigger boy say?

Child: He would probably say, "Move outta my way, I want to get a drink."

Mom: If there were other people in line, what do you think they would be thinking?

Child: "Fight, fight, fight!"

Mom: How do you think the smaller boy feels when he is pushed?

Child: Hurt. I mean . . . well, he's angry.

Mom: How is the bigger student feeling?

Child: Pushy.

Mom: Do you think it's okay to push somebody out of the way like that?

Child: I guess so.

Mom: What would make him stop?

Child: Um . . . maybe if the principal comes by.

Mom: Do you think the smaller student is being respected?

Child: No.

Mom: If he doesn't like being pushed, what should he do?

Child: He should tell the big kid to stop it, and if that doesn't work he should tell an adult.

Mom: If he told a teacher about being pushed, what might happen to the big kid?

Child: He could get punished, in a way. Maybe suspension, but maybe like free time taken away.

Mom: If the big kid got in trouble, what might happen to the small student?

Child: He might get hurt again because he told . . . if the big kid found out.

Mom: He might. Has anything like this ever happened at school? Or to anybody at school?

Child: Nope. I don't think so. Not that I know of.

Lessons Learned from This Sample Talk

In this discussion, the child finally determines that it is disrespectful to push other children around. The parent might want to follow up with more questions about who, specifically, the child should tell and how soon after witnessing the pushing he should speak up. The parent might also ask why the big kid thinks it's okay to push around smaller children. The child says he has not seen any pushing at school, which is unlikely given the typical behavior of elementary school children. Later talks and further probing might reveal that he has witnessed similar incidents. The parent might ask: How would you feel if you were pushed to the ground by another student? How do you feel when you see people pushed or hit?

Discussing the Story about Threatening a Boy

Participants: a mother and her fourth-grade son.

Mom: I'm going to read this story to you. There is a new student at school. He is just leaving the cafeteria when he is approached by a group of guys. One of them says, "You made fun of me in class." The new student is confused. He doesn't know what the bigger kid is talking about. The group of guys look like they are going to hurt him. What is the new student thinking?

Child: He thinks, "What are you talking about?"

Mom: What is the bigger student thinking?

Child: That he's gone too far talking and he's really mad.

Mom: Okay. What is the new student saying?

Child: He says, "I don't know what you're talking about."

Mom: Okay. What is the bigger student saying?

Child: "You think you are so smart!"

Mom: And what are the other students thinking? Remember there's a group of guys that look like they're going to hurt the new student.

Child: They're probably really mad because the new boy was making fun of their friend.

Mom: Is there anything unusual happening in this situation?

Child: No.

Mom: What do you think could happen to the new student?

Child: He could get hurt badly or he could just run.

Mom: Okay. If the new student is hurt, what can he do?

Child: He could tell the principal.

Mom: If the new student tells a teacher about what happened, what might the bigger student do?

Child: He might get really mad at the new student and start picking on him after school.

Mom: Okay. Has anything like this ever happened at school? To you?

Child: Yes, once.

Mom: Like what? What happened?

Child: When? I forget. Someone was bothering me.

Mom: Yes? You want to explain that?

Child: No.

Mom: No? Okay. What would the kids who are watching this situation do? Like if you were one of the new student's friends?

Child: I would help the new student out.

Mom: How would you help him?

Child: By making sure they don't get into a fight.

Mom: And how could you do that?

Child: By stopping them.

Mom: How? How could you stop people from fighting?

Child: By saying, "Guys, there's no point in fighting. He might have made fun of you by accident. Whoopee do. He's still a person. He didn't kill anyone."

Lessons Learned from This Sample Talk

In this sample talk, the child acknowledges that he has experienced harassment of the type portrayed in the story. This can lead to reflection on the important lessons learned during this situation. After this experience, the child has empathy for the "victim" and was willing to intervene on his behalf. The parent may want to follow up with a discussion about what to do when the child feels like intervening may not be a safe thing to do. The mom did not probe further when the son said he did not want to discuss the time he was harassed. This was an important example of respecting personal boundaries. This does not mean the parent cannot revisit the talk later to get more information about what kind of harassment he experienced.

6

A Safer City

Talking about Violence in the Neighborhood

When I was ten, my father let me take the subway by myself for the first time. He took a map of the city and a highlighter, and he marked out huge areas. "Don't go here, or here, or here," he said, and that was that.—Henry, father of three, Boston

I asked my son what his new friend's parents did for a living. He said his friend's dad was a doctor who was in prison for attempting to murder his wife. That comment suddenly changed my view of my neighborhood.—Patrice, mother of two, Seattle, Washington

I'm reading the newspaper about a high school student who supposedly had good grades, went to church with his grandmother and suddenly went into a rage in the subway, slashing people's faces with a knife. Then I read another story about a guy who pushed a woman in front of a train but wasn't convicted of murder because he's insane. Now I'm supposed to go uptown with my daughter on the subway.—Maria, mother of two, New York City

Your child's world grows as she grows older. During early elementary school, a child's life takes place in the home, the school, and wherever the parent may go. By fourth grade, lots of kids start going out on their own to a neighbor's house or on trips to the movies. By middle school, many young people want to experiment with independence and seek more free, unsupervised time away from parents. Their world includes the entire neighborhood, the neighbors' homes, sports fields, city centers, and malls. By the time teens enter high school, their world can be as large as that of their peers or other adults. How safe is your child as her world expands? What skills will she need to navigate her neighborhood and the complex relationships she finds there?

Preparing for the Talk

The talk in this chapter will give you a chance to discuss how your child feels about her world, apart from school and home life. This talk is about giving your child the critical thinking skills to navigate potentially dangerous situations, whether walking down the street, riding on a bus, or spending time at a friend's house. This talk opens the door for ongoing conversations that you can have with your child as her neighborhood expands and her life experience broadens.

In this talk you will let your child know that

- she can depend on you for support when facing any threats of violence from anyone in the neighborhood.
- there are crime prevention precautions that she can take.
- you have expectations about her behavior as she goes from home to school and to other destinations.
- there are family rules about violence and safety in the neighborhood.

What You Can Expect from This Talk

After the talk your child will

- be able to identify potentially violent situations in the neighborhood.
- understand that there are many forms of intimidation, harassment, and violence that can come from both strangers and neighbors.
- understand your family rules about violence and safety in the neighborhood.

How Safe Is Your Neighborhood?

Think about the following behaviors. Do they exist in your neighborhood?

- A person yells something cruel about a neighbor.
- Some older boys grab a boy's shirt and tell him he is "gonna be initiated into the neighborhood."
- A group of older boys hang out in the community center, flirting with and intimidating the younger girls.
- A big guy tells a child to hand over his money while he's on an errand to buy some groceries at the local store.
- A neighbor pulls out a gun to show off in front of other boys.
- Someone paints a swastika on your neighbor's front door.
- A dad down the block makes sexually suggestive comments to an eighth-grade girl who is baby-sitting his kids.
- On the bus, a man tries to rub up against a teenage girl.

Do you think the behaviors listed above involve violence or the threat of violence? In Chapter One we spent some time defining violence and threats of violence. For many parents, all of the behaviors listed above represent some form of potentially violent behavior. In this talk, there will be opportunities to discuss your point of view, how prevalent these behaviors are in your neighborhood, and what can be done about any problems.

When I was sixteen, I had a car accident and had to start using a wheelchair. The neighborhood changed in a lot of ways! My rehabilitation counselor told me I had to take self-defense classes—he said now that I'm in a wheelchair, I'll be seen as a target, since it's hard to fight back or get away. That was fifteen years ago—no problems yet.—Jeff, New York City

The Neighborhood Pecking Order

When I was in second grade, I was playing in my front yard and some older neighbor boys grabbed me and wrestled me to the ground. They slapped me and fondled me. They told me not to tell anybody or they would "get me." I never told my parents.—Rob, Seattle, Washington

Just as students at school establish a pecking order, so do the youth in neighborhoods. Much of this has to do with socioeconomic status or income levels, and some of it has to do with physical strength, race or ethnicity, sex roles, sexual orientation, or attractiveness. In some neighborhoods it might be the guy who has won the most fights, the kid with guns, or the wealthiest girl. Of course, some kids want to opt out of the neighborhood's "order" and be left alone. This is much easier said than done.

I wish I knew in high school what I know now. I would not have let the older boys who live around the block intimidate me. They never did anything to me; just the threat was enough.
—Sal, mother of three, Chicago

I grew up in an apartment complex and it was the older brothers of my friends who ran the place. At least it looked that way from my third-grade perspective. I was only slugged and pushed once but that was enough to tell me where I stood and to be cautious.
—Doug, New York City

Influence of the Media

In the 1950s, TV shows and news programs usually portrayed all crime as coming from outside of safe neighborhoods. Life was portrayed simplistically, with violent people coming from "across the tracks" to attack innocent middle-class families.

Today's TV shows and films show violence in all kinds of neighborhoods, from housing projects to Beverly Hills. The violence usually varies based on socioeconomics or income level. Violence among the working class or poor usually involves gangs or shoot-outs with police. Violence among the middle class or wealthy usually involves less visible forms of violence, like spousal abuse or child abuse. In some ways, we have the origin of the made-for-TV movie for showing the underbelly of suburban life—with the movie of the week focusing on alcoholic wife beaters, dads committing incest, or sociopathic teens who terrorize others. Only you can decide if your child is being exposed to news stories that are giving her distorted views of her neighborhood's violence.

Pressure from Peers

For most of us, fitting in is part of getting through the day. For children, finding acceptance from peers in their neighborhood is often of critical importance. You can remember how good it felt as a child to have neighborhood friends. Pressure to find a friend or group to play with probably increases as children move from elementary to middle to high school. As a parent, you can have influence over what kind of group your child spends time with. Meeting your child's friends and talking with them can give you clues about the values they have. Before your child spends time at a friend's home, it's perfectly reasonable to give the friend's parents a call to double-check on the visit.

I know where my sixth grader is all the time. I always talk with the parents of any child he is visiting in the neighborhood, as well as the teachers and coaches he spends time with. It always surprises me when my son's friends come over for dinner and none of their parents call to check on them.—Doris, mother of two, Long Island, New York

I grew up in Jacksonville, Florida. Before I could go visit a friend's home, my mom would ask, "What kind of people are your friend's parents? Are they church people?"
—Cheryl Boykins, Center for Black Women's Wellness, Atlanta, Georgia

Giving Your Child the Big Picture

I travel all over the country and work with all kinds of parent groups, from affluent suburbs to inner-city housing projects. I see the same problems everywhere. Many parents are working longer hours and have less time than ever to supervise their children. More and more families are headed by single moms, with little help from outside. And kids are spending many hours a day absorbing the violent messages of TV, films, and video games. Take poor supervision, weak emotional attachment to parents, and exposure to violence, and add poverty or academic failure, and you've got some of the key risk factors for violence among children. Lisa Perry, who spent years directing a community health education program in Seattle, Washington, offers the following insight on the connections between economic development and violence:

During my work with the Annie E. Casey Foundation, starting in 1995, our parent-child communication programs were offered in housing projects in Seattle, Atlanta, San Diego, New Orleans, and Hartford, Connecticut. The families in these communities face enormous challenges: poor housing, decades of unemployment or underemployment, few social services, and schools in disrepair. The talks in these communities were candid, thoughtful, and practical. Elementary-school children talked quite openly about seeing guns, and sometimes even experiencing abuse. It's disturbing to hear young girls talk about incest in such a matter-of-fact tone.

Parent-child communication alone won't save such a violent culture. Parent involvement, coupled with coordinated community involvement, targeted economic development through government programs, and long-term private-sector investment are what may turn these historically neglected neighborhoods around. We simply must address the needs of the children living there.

Violence occurs among all income groups. The suburbs may appear peaceful, but the truth is they offer no haven from violence or abuse.

∎

I grew up in an affluent suburb. And to me, every family looked happy. I was suffering at the hands of an abusive mother, but I thought I was the only one! It was only later that I realized how much of that was going on in the neighborhood. There was a lot of money there, and a lot of abuse and suffering, too—all of it in silence.
—Carrie, mother of one, Newport Beach, California

Different Families: Different Values

Your child is presented with many values about violence. You have your values and rules. But your child's friends, neighbors, and coaches may have different ones. The following scenarios illustrate how your child may receive different messages in his daily life.

To get from home to school a boy has to pass a group of older boys who yell threats at him.

Some neighborhood parents see this situation as part of life and something a guy simply has to deal with. Others might say he needs to "show what he's made of." If you don't intervene, is the message that guys have to deal with intimidation on their own?

∎

A dad is driving a teenage girl home after baby-sitting his kids. The dad repeatedly compliments the girl on her looks, saying she is devel-

oping into "a beautiful young woman." The girl feels both flattered and uncomfortable.

Some parents would find this man's behavior totally unacceptable. Others might see the man's actions as harmless flirting or good-natured complimenting. Is this also a situation that could lead to inappropriate physical behavior between the adult male and the young girl? Does a young person, male or female, need to be taught how to identify inappropriate adult behavior? What are the consequences of not discussing such behavior with your child?

■

A boy is attending a youth night at a local religious center. After the meeting, the boy and youth leader are alone talking. The older youth leader is touching the boy's knee. The boy is very uncomfortable but not sure why. The program leader has always been a nice guy.

Is this harmless affection or inappropriate touching? Perhaps the boy is feeling uncomfortable for a number of reasons. He may not be used to physical affection from another male. Or perhaps the older leader is crossing a line and not respecting the boy's personal boundaries. When a child, male or female, feels any kind of discomfort, it's important for him or her to say so. It is better to be overly cautious when expressing personal boundaries.

■

A girl is walking home at dusk from the neighborhood store. A nice-looking guy in a new car is following her. The guy rolls down his window and says, "Hi," and reminds the girl that he is the older brother of one of her friends from school. He asks her if she wants a ride home.

Some parents would say that the older brother of a school friend most likely is not a threat. Others would caution any girl about being alone with an older male she does not know well. Most parents tell their kids not to get into a stranger's car. But often it's not a stranger who poses the problem. Do you see any potential problems with the girl getting into the guy's car? (Could it be safer than walking alone in that neighborhood?)

The neighborhood dad, the older guys in the park, the church's youth leader, and the older brother of a school friend all may be familiar faces. And they all have their own values about whom they can touch, how they can touch, and when they can threaten violence. Certainly violence committed by strangers is a reality, and safeguarding your family from these potential crimes is part of being a parent. However, in most cases of molestation or inappropriate touching, the victimizer is known by the victim. The goal is to give your child the skills to recognize potentially dangerous behaviors, whether from strangers or persons with whom she is familiar.

Last-minute Checkups before the Talk

Before the talk, think about how safe you felt in your neighborhood when you were a child.

- Did your parents tell you to expect some violent behavior in the neighborhood?
- Did they insist that you not talk to strangers?
- Did they tell you a child must always be polite and respectful to adults?

- Did they talk to you about the difference between safe and inappropriate touching?

How about your child today?

- How safe does she feel walking to and from school, or waiting at the bus stop?
- Have you told her to expect some threats or harassment from the neighborhood kids and adults?
- Have you taught her the difference between safe and inappropriate touching?
- Have you discussed when it's permissable to put manners aside in favor of safety?

Do you have any stories about growing up and dealing with violence in your neighborhood? For example:

- A story about a neighbor who threatened you
- An experience with a stranger confronting you
- A time when an adult you trusted tried to touch you in a way that was inappropriate
- A story about how you called the police to report a crime

Your child can benefit from hearing how you faced these situations and developed confidence.

What Are Your Family Rules?

Do you have family rules about safety in the neighborhood? If not, this is a good time to think about them. The talk outlined in this chapter highlights the following situations:

- Problems at a bus stop
- A girl setting boundaries with a man
- A man touching a girl without permission
- Boys intimidating another boy at the pool
- Children seeing drug dealers on the street corner

Addressing these situations will give you an opportunity to discuss your family rules about dealing with potential problems in the neighborhood. What would you want your child to do in each situation? What are your expectations? What family rules do you have, or can you put in place, to address these situations? Before the talk, think about what rules you want to communicate to your child. At the end of this chapter you will have the opportunity to review these family rules together.

The Talk

Introduce the Talk

With this book in hand, tell your child: "I need you for about five minutes to talk about some safety rules." Once you have secured a quiet five minutes you may proceed by asking, "First, can you give me some examples of violence in this neighborhood?"

Your child may offer some examples. They may be similar to the behaviors described at school. If so, proceed with the next section.

If he doesn't offer examples of violence, say something like, "There are many different kinds of violence, some small and some big. When boys fight at the school bus stop, can that be a form of violence? Or do you call it 'playing'? Life-threatening violence takes many forms including: when someone is carjacked, attacked, raped, robbed, or shot. Some neighborhoods have a lot of violence, while others have less."

If you feel that your child needs to review the definition of violence, you can offer the following examples: any unwanted touching, pushing, name-calling, threats of violence, intimidation, or a fist, knife, or gun waved in a threatening way.

Review These Words

Please review the terms in this section. Discussing all the terms with your child is optional. You know what's appropriate for your child's age and maturity level. More than likely, even the youngest children have heard these words on TV.

community: the people living in a common location. Neighborhoods are communities. Some communities are very active and bring families together for street fairs and educational and political events. Neighborhoods with a strong sense of community are often safer places to live.

crime rate: how much crime is happening in a certain state, city, or neighborhood. The police department usually has these figures.

Neighborhood Watch: a program operated by many police departments to help neighbors develop strategies for reducing crime and suspicious activities in their neighborhood. The neighbors agree to look out for each other and report suspicious activities to the police.

911: the number to call when you have an emergency. It can be called to report threatening activity, crime, fire, or medical emergencies.

police report: When there is a crime or a threat of a crime, the police write out a report to document the problem.

Why Is Talking about Violence in the Neighborhood Important?

Let your child tell you why she thinks talking about violence in the neighborhood is important. Here are some additional reasons you might want to include:

- Talking about violence means learning to identify potentially violent behavior and how to prevent it before it happens.
- Talking about violence in the neighborhood helps us know where to get help (the police, social workers, religious groups, and crime watch group). It is also an opportunity to talk about making the neighborhood a safe, community-minded place.
- Talking about violence means clarifying family rules on keeping safe in the neighborhood.

The Stories

In the next part of the talk, you'll be reading short stories to your child and discussing them together. You don't have to read all of the stories. Pick the ones that you think are appropriate for your child. The stories are very simple. Feel free to embellish them, adding details that you think might make the story more believable to your child.

The Story about Waiting for the Bus

This story provides an opportunity to discuss how to respond to threats of violence and situations in which it might not be appropriate or safe for an observer to intervene. You and your child can talk about how to report violent behavior.

"A boy is waiting for the school bus. A group of older boys starts to call him names and shove him."

The discussion questions that follow will allow you to find out how your child feels about intimidation and threats of violence.

Ask these questions of your child:

- What do the older boys say?
- What does the younger boy say?
- What are the older boys thinking?
- What is the younger boy thinking?

Now that your child has completed this scenario, ask the following questions:

- Is this an example of a threat of violence? Why?
- Is this an example of violence? Why?
- How often does this really happen?
- Have you ever seen or been in a situation like this? If so, how did you feel? What did you do?

- What would be the best thing to do if you were being threatened in a situation like this?

Clarify Your Family's Values

Discuss these questions with your child as a way of sharing your values about violence in the neighborhood. We have included a number of potential responses from children to help you formulate your own responses.

Ask your child: "If a person is threatened with violence by a group of guys, what can that person do?"

Child response #1: Run.
Parent: Right. That might be a great idea. Where can they run to? What else can a person do?

Child response #2: Fight back.
Parent: Yes, that might be an option. It depends on the situation. Let's talk about self-defense—how you can learn it and what it means.

Child response #3: Tell somebody.
Parent: Right. If you ever feel threatened in any way, you can tell me. Together we can figure out what to do.

Child response #4: Join a gang to have protection.
Parent: I know that some people feel that joining a gang is a way to survive. What are other ways to deal with threats of violence in the neighborhood that don't involve joining a gang?

The Story about the Girl Walking Home

This story will give you a chance to discuss unwanted attention and ways to get the victimizer to stop.

"A girl is walking home from the store. An older boy walks up to her and starts talking to her, telling her how good she looks. She does not know the boy. He starts to touch her face."

Ask these questions of your child:

- What is the older boy saying?
- What is the girl saying?
- What is the older boy thinking?
- What is the girl thinking?

The discussion questions that follow will allow you to find out how your child feels about flirting, harassment, intimidation, respecting personal boundaries, and threats of violence.

Now that your child has completed this scenario, ask the following questions:

- Is this an example of a threat of violence?
- Is this an example of violence?
- What could the girl do to make the boy go away?
- Have you seen or been in a situation like this? If so, how did you feel? What did you do?
- What would be the best thing to do if you were being threatened in a situation like this?

187

Clarify Your Family's Values

Discuss these questions with your child as a way of sharing your values about violence in the neighborhood.

Ask your child: "What can a girl do when a person is bothering her?"

Child response #1: Yell, "Leave me alone!"
Parent: Talking is better than yelling. But sometimes you just have to yell if the person won't stop and you need help.

Child response #2: Just ignore him as much as possible.
Parent: Yes, you could try ignoring him. Sometimes you have to remove the guy's hand if he's touching you. You control who can touch you. And if you want to know about self-defense classes I will talk with you about finding one.

Child response #3: I don't know.
Parent: Let's talk about our family rules about how to deal with people who bother you.

The Story about the Girl in the Car

This story gives you a chance to talk about unwanted attention from adults the child knows well. Victimizers are often people the child is at least acquainted with.

"A neighborhood dad is driving a girl home after she has spent the evening baby-sitting his kids. He starts to tell her how pretty she is and places his hand on her knee. She feels very uncomfortable."

Ask these questions of your child:

- What is the man saying?
- What is the girl saying?
- What is the girl thinking?
- What is the man thinking?

Now that your child has completed this scenario, ask the following questions:

- Is this an example of a threat of violence? Why?
- Is this an example of violence? Why?
- What should the girl do?
- Why would the man do something like that?
- What happens if the girl tells the man to stop touching her and he doesn't?
- Have you ever seen or been in a situation like this? If so, how did you feel? What did you do?
- What would be the best thing to do if you were being threatened in a situation like this?

Clarify Your Family's Values

Discuss these questions with your child as a way of sharing your values about violence in the neighborhood.

Ask your child: "When a trusted adult tries to touch another person without permission, can it involve a threat of violence?"

Child response #1: I don't know.

Parent: It could lead to threats of violent behavior. Can you see how that could happen?

Child response #2: Maybe.

Parent: Adults touching children in any sexual or sexually suggestive way is not healthy. What might happen to the girl if she says nothing about being touched?

Child response #3: What do I do if a person tries to touch me?

Parent: Tell him to stop. Push his hands away from your body. If you want to talk about learning self-defense to help you in these situations let me know.

The Story about Boys at the Swim Center

This story gives you an opportunity to discuss threatening behavior by older boys and how to avoid it. You can also review the kinds of situations in which your child should seek adult assistance.

"A boy is at the swimming center. He's ready to go home, but when he enters the shower area, two older teenage boys are sitting on the bench smoking cigarettes, talking loudly, and rolling up their towels and whipping the lockers with them. The boy wants to take a shower and change into dry clothes, but the older teenagers are blocking his way."

Ask these questions of your child:

- What is the younger boy saying?
- What are the teenagers saying?
- What is the younger boy thinking?
- What are the teenagers thinking?

Now that your child has completed this scenario, ask the following questions:

- Is this an example of a threat of violence? Why?
- Is this an example of violence? Why?
- What should the boy do?
- Why would the teenagers act like that?
- What happens if the boy asks the teenagers to move and they don't move?
- Have you ever seen or been in a situation like this? If so, how did you feel? What did you do?
- What would be the best thing to do if you or someone you know were in a situation like this?

The Story about the Dealers on the Corner

This story gives you a chance to talk about situations that your child should try to avoid, and circumstances that should be reported to the police.

"A boy and girl are walking home from school. They come across two older teenage boys standing on the corner dealing drugs."

Ask these questions of your child:

- What is the younger boy thinking?
- What is the younger girl thinking?
- What are the teenage boys thinking?
- What are the teenage boys saying?

Now that your child has completed this scenario, ask the following questions:

- Is this an example of a threat of violence? Why?
- Is this an example of violence? Why?
- What should the boy or girl do?
- Have you ever seen or been in a situation like this? If so, how did you feel? What did you do?
- What would be the best thing to do if you or someone you know were in a situation like this?

Clarify Your Family's Values

Discuss these questions with your child as a way of sharing your values about drug dealing in the neighborhood.

Parent: "When you see older people selling drugs on the street, can it involve a threat of violence?"

Child: "I don't know."

Parent: "Well, selling drugs is illegal. If there's a conflict between a drug dealer and a buyer, they can't call the police, can they? They have to resolve it themselves, often through violence.

Can you see how this kind of violence could affect other people in the neighborhood?"

The Bare Minimum: A Quick Quiz for Kids

Ask your child the following questions to assess her knowledge of the many forms of violence that can happen in the neighborhood.

1. What are common forms of violence in this neighborhood? Sample answers:
- hitting at the school bus stop, threats from older kids, intimidation by bigger kids, shoving at the park

2. Sometimes a person in the neighborhood can touch a child in ways that make her feel uncomfortable. Sometimes this touching is a show of affection. Sometimes it's not supposed to happen. How do you know if the touching is wrong and unsafe? Sample answer:
- If a person is touched in any way that makes her uncomfortable, then it is wrong. A child should always report unsafe touching to a parent or trusted relative. This is true if the person doing the touching is a friend, a friend's parents, a relative, a worker at the park, or someone at the religious center. Even if a friend of a parent has made a child uncomfortable—the parent wants to know about it.

Talk about Your Family Rules

These rules are similar to the rules in Chapter One, but they can always use reinforcing.

What is our family rule about hitting others?
Sample answers:
- We never hit anyone.
- We don't threaten people with violence of any kind.
- We use force only in self-defense or to get away from a violent situation.

What is a family rule about reporting any threats of violence?
Sample answers:
- If you feel threatened in any way by anyone, I want to hear about it.
- If you feel unsafe in any way, I want you to tell me about it.
- If for some reason you feel like you can't tell me about threats, then you will tell the other adults we have agreed upon. (Give your child the name of a trusted relative or friend.)

What is our family rule about being touched by anyone, whether strangers or neighbors?
Sample answers:
- If it makes you uncomfortable, then I should hear about it.
- Don't be afraid to yell "Stop" if you feel you have been touched inappropriately.

What is our family rule about contacting the police?
Sample answer:
- We call 911 when it is an emergency. (You may want to give examples of what you consider an emergency.)

After the Talk

A Moment to Reflect

Take a moment to reflect on the talk you just had with your child. How does your perception of your neighborhood compare to your child's?

- Does your child view your community as a safer or scarier place than you?
- What could you do to make your child feel safer in the neighborhood?
- Is there anything you and your neighbors could do to make the community safer?
- How much of the time would you say you were listening to your child?

Warning Signs

This talk may reveal potential problems that your child is facing in the neighborhood. There may be cause for concern if your child, during the course of the talk, said

- he is having to hide from threatening people or gangs in your neighborhood.
- she is giving away money or possessions to others out of fear for her safety.
- he feels like the boys and girls in the stories deserved to have violence inflicted upon them.
- he felt that in the stories with girls and unwanted touching, the

reality was that "the girls were asking for it" and the males weren't doing anything wrong.
- she doesn't feel that people have a right to control who touches them.

Trust your instincts. Children, especially older ones, enjoy acting out during these talks, especially if they know it will upset a parent. But the stories raise important issues and ethical concerns, and if your child refuses to participate in any of the talks or discuss the related issues seriously, there may be cause for concern. Check with a trusted family member or friend to talk about your child's behaviors and attitudes to see if they agree that your concerns are justified.

Finding Help

If needed, support and help for your child is available. One thing to consider is helping your child build confidence. Some parents have enrolled their kids in self-defense classes. There are many forms of classes to strengthen a child's self-esteem, confidence, and agility.

Success Stories

You have made it through talk number six. Reward yourself for a job well done. The stories parents hear in the course of this talk are as varied as their neighborhoods. One dad in the Bronx used the talk to discuss ways his young son could look out for himself on the street; the son even expressed interest in self-defense classes. One mom in Portland, Oregon, said her daughter refused to believe that an older man she was baby-sitting for would ever make sexual advances; by the end of the talk, the daughter was willing to acknowledge that it could happen. Together, the mother and daughter talked about how important it is for girls to stay aware in those situations. Whether the topic of your talk was self-defense or sexual harassment, realize that some of life's most important issues were on the table. And that's the biggest success of all.

Sample Talks

Between Parents and Children

If you are wondering how a talk based on this chapter might really sound, take a look at the following excerpts from real family talks.

Discussing the Story about Waiting for the Bus

Participants: a mother and her fifth-grade son.

Mom: A boy is waiting for the bus. A group of bigger boys start to call him names and shove him. What types of things are the bigger boys saying?
Child: "Look at the wimpy guy, he's so stupid. HA, HA, HA."
Mom: What does the smaller boy say?
Child: "SHUT UP!"
Mom: What are the bigger boys thinking when this happens?
Child: "Why should we shut up?"

Mom: Why are they picking on the little guy?

Child: Because they're doing what they do best. No, they're just doing what they feel like doing because they don't like him.

Mom: What is the smaller boy thinking while this is happening?

Child: "Oh, no."

Mom: Is this an example of a threat of violence? Why?

Child: They are actually pushing him. So it's not just a threat.

Mom: Is this an example of violence?

Child: Yes, if they are shoving him.

Mom: How often does this really happen?

Child: I don't know, five or ten times a year? I don't really know.

Mom: Have you ever seen or been in a situation like this?

Child: Well, I've seen them pushing, shoving, making fun, but not actually meaning it.

Mom: So you've seen it when people didn't actually mean to hurt anyone but they were just pushing each other around?

Child: Yeah, like this . . . (he pushes his mom gently).

Mom: Do you think the smaller kids ever feel threatened by this?

Child: Yeah.

Mom: Do you think that's because they don't know that the bigger kids don't mean to hurt them?

Child: Well the one that you're talking about, it seems that they do want to hurt.

Mom: Well yes. That's what this sounds like. What would be the best thing to do if you were in a situation like this?

Child: Either walk away, or if they don't let you, deal with it.

Mom: If you were the smaller boy, how would you deal with it?

Child: I don't know.

Mom: If you were an observer watching this whole thing, is there something you would do?

Child: If they actually started to punch or really hurt him, yes.

Mom: What would you do?

Child: Say, "Stop it. Pick on someone else."

Mom: Would you help if these were adults doing this, or would you help only if there were other kids doing this?

Child: Well, if I'm just a kid, then I wouldn't really be a match for the adults, but if they were kids, then maybe I could actually do something.

Mom: So you'd tell them to stop picking on him?

Child: If they start to hurt him.

Lessons Learned from This Sample Talk

In this talk, the child revealed that he would be thoughtful about getting involved and make the decision based on the size and age of those who were doing the threatening. The parents may want to expand this and provide some other situations to help the child further clarify his strategies for getting involved, especially since the risk of becoming the target exists if one tries to intervene. The parent can ask: How do you feel when you see people fighting? How would you feel trying to break up a fight? How would you feel if suddenly people ganged up on you if you tried to stop a fight?

Discussing the Story about the Girl Walking Home

Participants: a mother and her fifth grade daughter.

Mom: A girl is walking home from the store carrying a bag of groceries in her arms. A slightly older boy walks up behind her and starts talking to her. He moves in front of her, telling her how good she looks. He is starting to touch her face. What is the guy thinking?

Child: He's thinking, "She's pretty."

Mom: What do you think the girl is thinking?

Child: I think she's thinking, "Leave me alone. Don't bother me."

Mom: What is the guy saying?

Child: He's saying, "You're pretty, let's go out."

Mom: What do you think the girl is saying?

Child: "No, and quit following me."

Mom: Is this an example of the threat of violence?

Child: That could be.

Mom: Is this an example of violence?

Child: It could be.

Mom: If the guy keeps bothering her, what could the girl do to express her interest in being left alone?

Child: She could walk faster or just ignore him.

Mom: Have you seen or been in a situation like this?

Child: No.

Mom: What would you do if you were?

Child: I would say, "Leave me alone."

Lessons Learned from This Sample Talk

In this talk, the stage has been set for the parents to ask the child whom she would seek out to get away from the guy. This would provide an opportunity for the mom and child to do some joint problem solving. What can make this situation complicated is if the girl thought the guy was attractive and nice. She might have mixed feelings about being complimented but feel somewhat uncomfortable if the guy is too aggressive. This dynamic can also be explored in further talks. It's very important to reinforce the girl's decision to tell her parents right away about the incident. The parent can ask: How would you feel if you were being flattered by an older person? Have you ever felt fearful of an older person?

Discussing the Story about the Girl in the Car

Participants: a mother and her eighth-grade daughter.

Mom: A neighborhood dad is driving a girl home after babysitting his daughter. He is starting to touch her leg in ways that make her uncomfortable, like patting her knee. What is the girl thinking?

Child: She's probably thinking, "What is this man doing?" and "How long will it take me to get home?"

Mom: What is the man thinking?

Child: I'm not sure what the man is thinking, he could be thinking many different things. He could be thinking, what else he could do to the girl or maybe about something wrong in his life that is making him do these things to her.

Mom: What is the girl saying?

Child: She's probably just confused, and she's either not saying anything because she's too embarrassed to say anything or she's telling him to stop.

Mom: What is the man saying?

Child: I'm not sure what he would be saying. I think he probably would laugh or just keep driving.

Mom: How is this an example of a threat of violence?

Child: Because he's doing something the girl doesn't want him to do.

Mom: What should the girl do?

Child: She should continue to say, "Stop" and if he doesn't stop tell him to pull the car over and walk the rest of the way.

Mom: What is the girl feeling?

Child: She's feeling embarrassed and used and she probably just wants to go home.

Mom: What happens if the girl tells the man to stop and he doesn't?

Child: Then when she gets home, she should tell her parents and have something happen to this man so it doesn't happen again.

Mom: Have you ever seen or been in a situation like this?

Child: No.

Lessons Learned from This Sample Talk

This talk provided an opportunity for the child to think about what to do in an uncomfortable situation in which there is a power differential. Clearly, the young girl is at a disadvantage by being in a threatening situation with an older man. The parent can further explore the importance of being firm even when dealing with adults they assume they should be able to trust. The child mentioned that the girl in the story would feel "embarrassed." The parent might ask: Why would the girl feel embarrassed? Have you ever felt embarrassed in a similar situation?

Discussing the Story about the Girl in the Car

Participants: a mother and her fifth-grade son.

Mom: A neighborhood dad is driving a girl home after playing with his daughter. He is starting to touch her in ways that make her uncomfortable, like patting her knee. What is the girl thinking?

Child: Umm. She thinks, "What are you doing?"

Mom: What is the man thinking?

Child: I don't know.

Mom: What is the girl saying?

Child: "Will you please stop."

Mom: What is the man saying?

Child: "Stop doing what?"

Mom: So he's not even aware of what he's doing?

Child: No. He does not know what to stop. The patting or to stop the car.

Mom: Is this an example of a threat of violence?

Child: No.

Mom: What should the girl do if she doesn't like the man patting her?

Child: Tell him, "Would you please stop patting my leg," and if he doesn't stop then say, "Okay, just drop me off here."

Mom: That's a good idea. Why would the man do something like that?

Child: I don't know.

Mom: What happens if the girl tells the man to stop and he doesn't stop?

Child: Yell, "Drop me off here!"

Mom: Have you ever seen or been in a situation like this, where someone touched you when you didn't want to be touched?
Child: What do you mean? Like play or what?
Mom: Like an adult says, "Oh, give me a hug."
Child: Yes.
Mom: Who's done that?
Child: You.
Mom: (Laughs) Anyone besides your mom?
Child: And my brother when he goes "Ahhh" (like a monster attack). But he's playing.

Lessons Learned from This Sample Talk

The son shows a sense of justice when discussing how the girl should respond to the dad's touching. However, the boy seemed to think that the dad didn't know if he should stop the unwanted touching or the car. This might have been said in humor, as lots of children occasionally use humor and sarcasm to deflect serious subjects, the parent still needs to stress that "no" means "no." Further talks might reveal if the son has experienced any unwanted touching (besides that of his mom and brother). The parent might ask: How does the girl in the story feel? How does it feel when you say "no" to being touched and people don't listen?

Discussing the Story about Boys at the Swim Center

Participants: a mother and her fifth-grade daughter.

Mom: Tom is at the swimming center. He's ready to go home but when he enters the shower area two teenage boys are sitting on the bench smoking cigarettes, talking loudly, and rolling up their towels and whipping the lockers with them. Tom wants to take a shower and change into dry clothes, but these boys are blocking his way. What is Tom thinking?

Child: I think Tom is thinking, "Look at these boys, they're acting like fools."

Mom: What are the teenagers thinking?

Child: The teenagers are thinking, "We're the coolest."

Mom: And they can do whatever they want?

Child: Yeah.

Mom: What is Tom saying?

Child: Nothing.

Mom: What are the teenagers saying?

Child: "Go away."

Mom: Is this an example of a threat of violence?

Child: Yeah. It could be threatening, because they could hit him with a towel instead of hitting the lockers.

Mom: Or they could get out of control. What should Tom do?

Child: Tom should either push on by and go to the showers or he should go out and tell someone, "There's teenage boys in there bothering me, will you help me?"

Mom: How is Tom feeling?

Child: I think Tom is feeling really scared that these teenage boys might come and hurt him.

Mom: Why would the teenagers act like that?

Child: I think the teenagers would act like that because they don't really care about anything.

Mom: What happens if Tom tells the teenagers to move and they don't move?

Child: I think the teenagers would get pretty mad if Tom

told them to move. They would tell him to shut up and hit him.

Mom: Then I think Tom should go and get help, right?

Child: Yeah.

Mom: Have you ever seen or been in a situation like this?

Child: No.

Mom: Or a bully situation?

Child: No.

Mom: If you were, what would you do?

Child: I would just ignore it or I would go tell the aide at recess.

Mom: What would be the best thing to do if you or someone you knew were in a situation like this?

Child: Go tell someone.

Lessons Learned from This Sample Talk

In this talk, even though the child had never been in a situation like this, she was clear about the alternatives she would take. It's important to note that this was a girl coming up with options for a boy dealing with older boys. Daughters talk about being terrorized in the school bathroom by groups of girls. If you are talking with a son, you may find very different responses. Boys often rationalize such threatening behavior and accept bullying in silence. The reality is that in some neighborhoods, the pecking order reigns and the strong do rule the smaller and weaker kids. Many boys and men still feel like all males somehow have to "pay their dues" and "fight their own battles." This is something to discuss with both sons and daughters. Further talks might explore what happens when older guys start hitting you and how to respond.

7

Different Targets

Talking about Weapons

I would no more think of having a gun in my home than a hand grenade.—Esther, mother of three, Memphis, Tennessee

I collect a wide variety of vintage World War I and II handguns and rifles. My kids know that they are not to be touched.
—Steve, father of two, Jamestown, New York

My father was a police officer so we always had a gun in the house when I was growing up. We all knew where it was kept, but we also knew we weren't supposed to get into that cabinet. I never thought anything about it. Now, having a gun in one's home seems like more of an issue.—Karen, mother of two, Portland, Oregon

Weapons come in many forms, from guns to bows and arrows. Soldiers use weapons to wage war; police use weapons to keep order; hunters use weapons to kill game; and people with little regard for human life use weapons to express their rage, fear, and frustration. What kinds of weapons does it make sense for your child and his schoolmates to have easy access to? When, if ever, is it appropriate for your child and her friends to use weapons? Who is best equipped to teach your child how to use weapons safely? What are ways to prevent weapons from getting into the hands of people who might use them to hurt you or your child?

Preparing for the Talk

Parents have very different values when it comes to children using weapons. Some of their children live in your neighborhood and go to school with your child. This talk will give you and your child an opportunity to discuss your beliefs about using weapons.

In this talk you will let your child know that

- she can depend on you for support when talking about weapons.
- you have expectations about his use of weapons.
- there are family rules about weapons and safety.

What You Can Expect from This Talk

After this talk your child will

- be able to identify threats of illegal weapon use.
- understand the importance of safe and legal weapon use.
- understand the family rules about using weapons of any kind.
- know where to go for help if he has problems with someone using a weapon illegally or in a threatening way.

About Weapons

In this chapter, when we talk about weapons, we're talking primarily about guns. Weapons are a big industry in the United States, one that caters to a diverse market. The following data illustrate the prevalence of guns.

Proportion of U.S. households with a gun: 39%
(Source: Johns Hopkins Center for Gun Policy and
Research, National Opinion Research Center.
1997/98 National Gun Policy Survey:
Questionnaire with Weighted Frequencies)

Year in which gunfire injury is projected to surpass car accidents as the leading cause of traumatic death in the United States: 2001
(Source: Annals of Emergency Medicine (1998; 32: 51-59),
"Trends in nonfatal and fatal firearm-related injury rates in the
United States, 1985-95")

Amount of time that passes before a new handgun is produced in the United States: 12 seconds
(Source: U.S. Bureau of Alcohol,
Tobacco and Firearms Estimate, 1994)

Proportion of middle-school students who say they daydream about owning a gun: 27%
(Source: The Just Kid, Inc./Porter Novelli, 1999 Kid ID Study)

Proportion of elementary school students expelled for bringing firearms to school: 9%
(Source: U.S. Department of Education, 1998)

Proportion of students who say they know someone who's brought a gun to school: 12.7%
(Source: National Center on Education Statistics, Violence and
Discipline Problems in U.S. Public Schools, 1996-97)

Perspectives on Guns

Parents differ greatly in their views on guns. Some parents enjoy hunting as a sport and raise their children to do the same. They treat gun and rifle use as a serious sport demanding discipline, responsibility, and thoughtful conduct. Other parents don't like the idea of hunting animals, yet feel that having a gun in the house is part of good crime prevention. Still other parents abhor the idea of using a gun for any reason. They see gun use as too prevalent and would prefer that it be strictly regulated as it is in Western Europe, Canada, and Japan. It's up to you to make your own decisions about whether you will allow firearms in your home. Because of easy access to guns, it's important for you to talk with your child about what he should do if he sees one in your home, in a neighbor's home, or in the hands of a person on the street or at school.

To prepare for the talk, think back to your childhood and to your first encounter with guns, whether in real life or on TV. Consider the reflections of the following parents as they look back on their childhood experience with guns.

I remember my dad going pheasant hunting. We were taught never to even go near his gun. My parents were very strict about enforcing this rule with my brothers and me.
—Sally, mother of three, Denver, Colorado

A friend of the family had a son who was showing off a pistol to a high school friend. This kid knew how to handle guns, but there was a freak accident and he was killed.
—Linda, mother of two, Memphis, Tennessee

Our family loved hunting. As a kid I went to gun safety classes and we were taught basically not to aim at anything unless we were intent on killing it.—Brad, New York City

I never saw a gun until I joined the navy after high school. I was taught to shoot a gun. I was scared of the damn thing. I didn't know the first thing about guns, but I got more comfortable with it once I learned it had so many safeties. I don't think I could have shot anyone unless maybe it was to save another person's life.
—Pam, mother of two, Gaithersburg, Maryland

I was in college ROTC when I fired my first rifle. I thought it was cool.
—Jim, father of two, Rockville, Maryland

Influence of the Media

What does your child know about guns and other weapons? If he watches TV, he has probably been exposed to thousands of movies and news reports about guns, school shootings, and gun accidents. He and his peers have seen thousands of people killed on TV shows and countless films about police, FBI, SWAT teams, soldiers, and serial killers—all with guns. How does a child interpret these images? How does he separate the real horrors of a school shooting from the simulated massacres seen daily on TV? In the course of the talk, you may be able to find out.

Exposure to Weapons

Your child may play with toy guns, lasers, or soldiers and begin to see weapons as a normal part of life. Depending on where you live, the school your child is attending, and the friends he hangs out with, the pressure to use guns will vary. For younger children, using guns for protection is not the norm, although they may be aware that older siblings are using them. Some children may go to target practice with a parent to learn how to use a pistol.

Children are exposed to weapons in a variety of ways: seeing dad's hunting rifles, watching mom clean the pistol that she keeps near the bed for self-defense, watching an older sibling carry a hidden gun to take care of some business in a desolate part of town. Only you know what kinds of weapons your child is being exposed to and in what context they are supposed to be used. When you were growing up, how aware of guns were you and how comfortable were you in discussing their use with someone you trusted?

As a child, I saw a picture of my mom at a shooting range firing a pistol. I never understood what she was doing with a gun because she was an elementary schoolteacher. It seemed strange but I never felt I could ask her about the picture or guns until I was an adult.
—Robert, father of one, New York City

I grew up in a family that had lots of guns. We were taught how to use them at a very early age. They were for self-defense and they made my mom and dad feel safer.
—Jim, father of three, Jamestown, New York

I was once attacked by a guy. I was able to fight him off but I was beaten up pretty bad. I was so angry after that happened. If I had had a gun I might have blown his head off.
—Susan, mother of two, Rockville, Maryland

Giving Your Child the Big Picture

"Why did they shoot those kids?" asked a fifth grader after the school shootings in Littleton, Colorado. This is a question many children ask every time a school shooting makes the news. And it's a good question. First, they want to know why anybody would kill someone and what possibly could have caused the person to do it. They are looking to make sense out of the shooting—to see some logic in it. Some children even wonder how the shooter got the weapons.

Many people, young and old, don't realize how accessible guns and rifles are. The equivalent of swap meets for guns and rifles allows people in almost every city to buy, trade, and sell guns as easily as you would a used sweater. If you want to buy a gun from a gun store, you have to go through an FBI background check. This means that you give your name and other information to the store staff, who check to see if you legally can buy a gun. If the background check keeps you from getting approval, you can go to a gun swap meet and buy a gun without a background check.

One Dad's Story

Like a lot of kids who grew up in a big city, Cliff, a warm-hearted husband and devoted father of one, has some personal insight on the prevalence of guns in some children's daily lives. As you read this story, notice how many times Cliff encountered guns when he was growing up. How was your childhood different from Cliff's? Imagine how many children around the country are having childhoods like this right now.

I was six and our family had just moved into a new apartment in the Bronx. I remember looking at all the moving boxes and seeing two guys come in with guns and rob my parents. That was the first time I saw a gun.

When I was in fourth grade, I was walking down the street in front of my house when I saw two guys about sixteen years old. One says, "I heard you been messin' with my friend." He nods to his buddy. I was thinking, "What's he talking about? I don't know his friend." Then he punched me and both guys walked away. I sat there thinking, "What the hell was that all about?" I also thought that he might have had a gun.

When I was a freshman in high school, I was walking home from school when I saw a guy in his twenties with a gun chasing another guy. I heard shots. I ran the other way.

When I was a junior in high school, I was walking down the street and I looked into a grocery store. A guy was pointing a gun at the clerk. I ran as the police arrived.

During my senior year in high school I was in a car with friends at night. I looked out the window and saw a car pulling up next to us and two barrels of a shotgun pointed at us. I yelled out, "This guy's got a gun—get going!" My friend hit the pedal and we took off.

A year ago, I was going home to my wife and baby when two guys followed me into my building and then to the elevator. I could tell they didn't belong in the building. One guy pulled out a gun and said, "Gimme your money."

Different Families: Different Values

Everyone defines acceptable weapon use in his or her own way. Here are some behaviors that may be experienced differently depending on a person's background:

A brother threatens to shoot his toy gun at his sister.

Some parents see this as normal, healthy child's play, while others forbid a child to play with or point a toy gun at anyone.

■

A sixth grade boy shows his friend a knife that he has in his pocket. He's proud that he has had it all through the school day.

Some parents think a pocketknife is a helpful thing to carry, while others think a knife could be used as a weapon or to threaten others and shouldn't be brought to school. It is illegal in most states.

■

A seventh grader shows off his father's gun to a friend.

Some parents have no problem with a son showing a gun to a friend as long as it is not loaded, and is handled carefully. Others don't want their children around guns, loaded or unloaded, and would want their child to leave any home the moment a gun appeared.

■

A child overhears a phone conversation between her single mom and her mom's boyfriend. The mom is angry and says, "I don't want you coming over here anymore. I have my gun, so stay away."

Some parents might excuse this statement as something said in the heat of anger. Others view this kind of language as dangerous and inappropriate. It can be viewed as a real threat and a warning sign of potential violence that may escalate.

Last-minute Checkups before the Talk

Before the talk, it helps to think back to how you felt about guns when you were a child.

- Were there guns in the house?
- If so, were they used for hunting, self-protection, or both? Were they stored safely? Were you shown how to use them safely and legally?
- Did anyone ever threaten a family member with a weapon?

Are there guns in your house today?

- If so, does your child know where they are? Have you shown him how to use them safely and legally?
- Does your child spend time worrying about the threat of gun use?

This is a good time to think about your first childhood experiences with guns and other weapons. Do you have any stories that you can share with your child? For example:

- Watching a relative clean or maintain a gun
- Dealing with someone threatening you with a weapon of any kind
- Using a weapon

What Are Your Family Rules?

Do you have family rules about using guns, knives, or other weapons? If not, this is a good time to think about them. The talk outlined in this chapter highlights the following situations:

- A boy showing a knife to another child
- A boy playing with a gun
- A girl who suspects a student is using explosives
- A man and woman visiting a gun store
- A woman considering buying a gun for self-defense

Before you have your talk about guns and weapon use, consider spending some time reviewing the family rules you have in place. Are your rules working? It's important that your child has a clear understanding of the rules, why they are put in place, and the consequences of breaking them. At the end of the talk you will be able to review all the family rules about violence and safety in the home with your child.

The Talk

Introduce the Talk

If you are having these talks in sequence, you probably have practiced your opening lines more times than you care to remember. With this book in hand, tell your child: "I'd like to talk with you about weapons."

This may come as a big surprise to your child, especially if your family doesn't have a history of hunting or gun use.

You say, "What are some of the ways people use guns legally and safely?"

After identifying some examples, such as "when a dad has a hunting license and is shooting a deer in deer season. When a mom has a registered gun and goes to target practice to learn the correct way to shoot. When police officers or soldiers do their jobs."

After you talk about the legal and safe use of firearms, you may proceed with the next section.

Review These Words

Please review the terms in this section. Discussing all the terms with your child is optional. You know what's appropriate for your child's age and maturity level. More than likely, even the youngest children have heard these words on TV.

child safety locks: locks placed on gun triggers to keep a child from firing a gun.

concealed weapon: a weapon that is hidden. There are state and local laws about carrying a concealed weapon. Permits are required to carry concealed weapons in most places.

FBI background check: a federal law requires all gun stores to review the background of a person before a gun can be sold. This background check reviews the potential gun buyer's history with crime and related issues.

hunting license: a permit to hunt game.

hunting season: a time of the year when people can legally hunt game.

metal detectors: machines that are used in entrances to schools, airports, and other public buildings to spot guns or other weapons.

semi-automatic rifle: a rifle that can shoot many rounds of bullets without reloading.

shooting range: a place to practice using a gun.

Why Is Talking about Guns and Weapons Important?

Ask your child whether she thinks talking about guns and weapons is important. Here are some reasons you might want to offer:

- I know that there sometimes can be problems with people who use guns and other weapons.
- It is important for you to think about what you would do if you were in a situation where weapons were being handled.
- I want to make sure you know the rules about being around, holding, or using guns and other weapons.

The Stories

In the next part of the talk, you'll be reading short stories to your child and discussing them together. You don't have to read all of the stories. Pick the ones that you think are appropriate for your child. The stories are very simple. Feel free to embellish them, adding details that you think might make the story more believable to your child.

The Story about the Boy and His Knife

This story gives you a chance to review school and family rules about weapons.

"A boy is showing a girl a knife he brought to school."

Ask these questions of your child:

- What is the boy saying?
- What is the girl saying?
- What is the boy thinking?
- What is the girl thinking?

Now that your child has completed this scenario, ask the following questions:

- Might the boy use the knife in a violent way?
- What would stop the boy from using the knife in a violent way?
- What's a normal use for a knife?
- Has anything like this ever happened to you or to a friend?
- If so, how did you feel? What did you or your friend do?

Follow up with any questions you feel are appropriate given your child's responses.

The Story about a Boy Playing with a Gun

This story allows you to review gun safety rules and family rules about access to guns.

"An older boy is showing his friend his dad's new gun."

Ask these questions of your child:

- What is the older boy saying?
- What is his friend saying?
- What is the older boy thinking?
- What is his friend thinking?

Now that your child has completed this scenario, ask the following questions:

- Might the older boy want to use the gun?
- What would stop the older boy from using the gun?
- What should the friend do if the older boy wants to fire the gun?
- Has anything like this ever happened to you or to a friend?
- If so, how did you feel? What did you or your friend do?

Follow up with any questions you feel are appropriate, given your child's responses.

The Story about the Car Trunk

This story is about appropriate responses to suspicious or potentially threatening behavior.

"A girl is walking down the street. She passes a boy she has seen at school. He is a very quiet teenager with no friends and he gets teased a lot by some of the other kids. The boy is closing the trunk of his car. The girl passes the back of the car and catches a glimpse of what looks like firecrackers and wires. The boy seems nervous. It is February, not the Fourth of July."

Ask these questions of your child:

- What is the girl thinking?
- What is the boy thinking?

Now that your child has completed this scenario, ask the following questions:

- What is the girl going to do next? How might she feel?
- What could the boy have in his trunk besides firecrackers?
- What can happen if the boy is playing with explosives?

Follow up with any questions you feel are appropriate given your child's responses.

Stories for Older Children

The following stories are about buying guns. While some younger children may not be able to relate to them, you may find that to your child, these stories make perfect sense.

The Story about Buying a Gun

This story gives you the opportunity to talk with your child about why people buy guns, gun safety when children live in the house, and the process of buying a gun in your state.

"A man is at a gun store. He lives with his wife and two children. He is talking to the store clerk about wanting to buy a gun. The clerk is explaining the proper use of guns, how to safely store guns in a home with children, and the FBI background check."

Ask these questions of your child:

- What is the man saying?
- What is the clerk saying?
- What is the man thinking?

Now that your child has completed this scenario, ask the following questions:

- What kinds of questions should a person ask when buying a gun, especially if the person has children at home?
- What kinds of questions should the gun store clerk ask the man?
- How can the clerk be sure the man knows how to safely store the gun at home?

Follow up with any questions you feel are appropriate given your child's responses.

The Story about the Aunt's Decision

This story gives you a chance to talk with your child about why people buy guns, gun safety when children live in the house or visit the house, and the process of buying a gun in your state.

"A boy and girl's aunt is talking to the children's mom. The aunt will be moving to a big city in a few weeks and is worried about security. She is thinking about buying a gun and showing a magazine about guns to her sister."

Ask these questions of your child:

- What is the aunt saying?
- What is the mother saying?
- What is the aunt thinking?
- What is the mother thinking?

Now that your child has completed this scenario, ask the following questions:

- How does the son feel?
- How does the daughter feel?
- What would you do if you were the aunt?
- Are there ways to ease feelings of insecurity that don't involve buying a gun?

Follow up with any questions you feel are appropriate given your child's responses.

Clarify Your Family's Values

Discuss these questions with your child as a way of sharing your values about guns and other weapons. A number of potential responses from children are included to help you formulate your own responses.

> *Parent:* If a friend invited you over to his house while his parents were gone and he showed you his dad's new gun, what would I want you to do?
>
> *Child:* Run away.
>
> *Parent:* Yes. You wouldn't have to run, but I would want you to say that you have to go home and then come directly home.
>
> *Parent:* How do parents decide what their family rules about guns and weapons are?
>
> *Child:* I don't know.
>
> *Parent:* Rules are based on our experiences and our values. It's the parents' job to keep their children safe. But there are different points of view about how to keep a family safe. This is how I feel. (This is an excellent time to state your views on gun use for sports and self-protection.)
>
> *Parent:* What are the consequences of breaking family rules?
>
> *Child:* I don't know.
>
> *Parent:* When it comes to gun use we have very strict rules. It's literally a matter of life and death. If you break these rules, here are the consequences. (State your family's and the legal consequences.)

The Bare Minimum: A Quick Quiz for Kids

Ask your child the following questions to assess her knowledge of violence in the home.

1. Can you give me examples of safe and legal gun use?
   Sample answers:

- Hunting a deer in deer season.
- A police officer firing at a suspect in self-defense.
- Shooting at a firing range to practice the safe use of a licensed gun.

2. Can you give me some examples of unsafe ways to use a gun?
Sample answers:
- Kids are holding a loaded gun, without training or adult supervision.
- Kids are buying guns illegally from an older person who is breaking the law.
- A student is using a gun as a way of dealing with his frustration and anger.

Talk about Your Family Rules

This is an opportunity to review your family rules. Ask your child if he understands your family rules about guns and weapons.

1. What our are family rules about children using guns?
Sample answers:
- Children don't play with guns.
- Children don't show off guns to others.
- Children don't threaten people with guns or weapons of any kind.

2. What are the consequences of breaking the family rules about guns or weapons?
Sample answers:
- Time out or being grounded for a long time

- No TV, or TV removed from the bedroom
- No friends in the house or no phone calls
- No access to the computer for fun
- Meeting with a school counselor, social worker, or other professional

3. What are the legal consequences of using a weapon unlawfully? Sample answer:
- The police can become involved if guns or other weapons are misused. Severe consequences can occur if laws are broken.

After the Talk

After the talk about guns many parents report learning more about their child's views on playing with guns, buying weapons, or hearing about school shootings. Some parents were surprised to hear about incidents involving visiting a gun shop or using guns or knives. Others found that their child had definite views about how weapons should be used.

A Moment to Reflect

Take a moment to reflect on the talk you just had with your child.

- Do you feel that your child understands the life-and-death aspects of this topic?
- Were you concerned about anything you heard?

- Do you feel that you have family rules in place that help to keep your child safe in your home, or in other homes that she visits?
- Are you comfortable enforcing your family rules? If not, do you feel you can find the help you need?
- How much of the time were you listening to your child?
- Do you feel you might need to revisit some issues that came up during the talk?

Warning Signs

The talks also may reveal potential problems with your child. There may be cause for concern if you hear from your child that

- he doesn't appear to see anything wrong with using a gun unsafely.
- she doesn't see anything wrong with threatening a person with a gun.
- he thinks some family members or friends deserve to be hurt.
- she reveals an obsessive fascination with guns and other weapons.

If you get the sense that there might be a problem with your child and his views on weapons, don't hesitate to pursue the matter further. Use your intuition. This is a time when we have to take jokes about "blowing people away" seriously. Consider looking for outside help if you feel it might be warranted. Again, when it comes to weapons, it's better to be safe than sorry.

Finding Help

If this talk revealed what you consider to be a serious problem you may want to consider talking with a trusted family friend or trained counselor or therapist. You can call your local police department if you have questions about laws related to youth and gun use. There are many resources available in your community.

Success Stories

Congratulations on finishing talk number seven. Good job! Parents say this talk gave them a great opportunity to tell their kids what they should do if confronted with a gun—and whether you're an avid hunter or you've never touched a weapon, it's a vital topic in this country, where there are over 200 million guns in existence. Raising the topic is a success in itself.

Sample Talks

Between Parents and Children

If you are wondering how a talk based on this chapter might really sound, take a look at the following excerpts from real family talks.

Discussing the Story about a Boy Playing with a Gun

Participants: a single father and his fourth grade son.

Dad: An older boy is showing his friend his dad's new gun. What is the older boy saying?

Child: He's probably saying, "Ooh, look at my dad's new gun. Isn't it so cool. Do you want to shoot some bullets?"

Dad: And what is his friend saying?

Child: Well if it were a good friend, he'd say, "No you shouldn't play with that. Go take that back to your dad." But if it's a bad one, maybe like, "Sure, let's go in the woods and hunt for deer." Or something like that.

Dad: Might the older boy want to use the gun?

Child: Not me. I wouldn't want to use it. But if it were one of the kids who wanted to be cool, they would probably shoot it to show off.

Dad: What would stop the older boy from using the gun?

Child: His friend.

Dad: His friend would try to persuade him not to use it?

Child: Yeah. Tell him not to shoot it. If he doesn't listen to him, discourage him.

Dad: Discourage him and tell him he should put the gun away 'cause something bad might happen. You know how we've shown you in the paper and how you've seen in the news about guns. About people getting shot, either by accidents or by violent acts. When guns go to people who are careless with them or to people who are going to use them for violence, that's bad.

Child: They're only good when cops need them.

Dad: People have them for protection. Has anything like this ever happened to you or to a friend?

Child: Nope.

Dad: How would you deal with a situation like that, if one of your friends had a gun and was showing it to another friend? How would you deal with that?

Child: I wouldn't be his friend anymore.

Dad: Now, would you tell his mom? Who would you tell?

Child: Either his mother or his father.

Dad: So would you tell me first and have me tell his mother or father?

Child: I would take you with me.

Dad: Okay. It's important to have the parent involved.

Lessons Learned from This Sample Talk

The parent and child in the talk have been having talks all along about difficult topics that require making sound decisions. This talk has established that the son is clear in his pattern of seeking the help of an adult when confronted with a potentially violent situation. The child's good decision-making skills should be commended and the patterns of communication between parent and child reinforced in future talks. The parent might ask: How would you feel telling me about a friend of yours who was mishandling a gun?

Discussing the Story about the Car Trunk

Participants: a mother and her eighth-grade son.

Mom: This is a story about a very quiet teenager with no friends and who spends most of his time alone. He is getting out of his car in front of his home. A girl is walking down the sidewalk in front of the boy's house. The girl knows how smart he is at school but she also knows he gets teased a lot by some of the other kids. The girl sees the boy looking in his car trunk. He spots her and closes it quickly. She thinks she saw a lot of firecrackers and wires in his trunk. She wonders if he is making some kind of explosive device because it is February, not the Fourth of July.

Mom: What is the girl thinking?

Child: She thinks, "I have to ask him what he's doing."

Mom: What do you think he is going to say?

Child: If the girl asks him what's in the trunk he'll say, "What? I don't know what you are talking about."

Mom: Why do you think the boy had the firecrackers?

Child: Because he wants to get back at some people and maybe scare them.

Mom: How does the boy feel?

Child: He thinks it's the right thing to do because no one ever respects him.

Mom: What can be the result of the boy setting off the fireworks or combining them together into a very large explosive?

Child: He could be sent to jail or fined or something.

Mom: What could happen to people if he sets off an explosive?

Child: They could get hurt.

Mom: So do you think the girl should tell an adult what she saw?

Child: I guess so.

Mom: What kind of an adult should the girl talk to?

Child: Maybe a teacher or someone.

Lessons Learned from This Sample Talk

This child seemed to have a good understanding of what might motivate the boy to use the firecrackers, and the talk gave the mother the opportunity to point out the consequences and appropriate actions to take. The parent might want to stress the importance of telling a parent, in addition to a teacher, about such activity.

Discussing the Story about the Aunt's Decision

Participants: a father and his sixth-grade daughter.

Dad: A boy and girl's aunt is talking to the children's mom. The aunt will be moving to a big city in a few weeks and is worried about security. She is thinking about buying a gun. What is the aunt saying?

Child: I think the aunt is saying that when she moves to the city, she's going to be pretty scared. Maybe she has children and she wants to buy a gun for protection.

Dad: What do you think that the mom is saying?

Child: I think the mother is trying to tell her sister some advice. Maybe she should get some security systems or live in a different area.

Dad: What is the boy saying?

Child: I think the boy would be wondering why and, he'd be kinda curious and he'd just ask about the gun and want to see it and that could be a bad thing, maybe.

Dad: What is the girl saying?

Child: I think the girl is the mature one and she is just keeping it all calm inside. She'll just try to let it blow over like it's not bothering her.

Dad: It's not a good idea to the girl?

Child: Yeah, like the girl is saying, "Why does my aunt have to buy a gun? I mean, it's really dangerous. Cause if it's loaded, is she going to leave it out?" And her brother can get into it, maybe, so she's really scared about it.

Dad: He would be curious and want to shoot it at something?

Child: Yeah. I think he's, like, trying to get a hold of the gun, feel it, and say, "Oh wow, I'm holding the gun that my aunt has."

Dad: What do you think the girl is thinking to herself?

Child: She's thinking, "I don't want to do anything with the gun. Why did my aunt get a gun? She shouldn't have done that. She could have just moved somewhere else or something."

Dad: Right. But even if she lived in the city she wouldn't need a gun. A lot of people live in cities and they don't have guns. There are better ways, having locks on the door, an alarm system, going out during the daytime. There are ways of living in society without having to be fearful of going out without a gun.

Dad: What do you think the aunt is thinking?

Child: I think she's thinking that she bought it for a good cause.

Dad: For self-defense? To protect herself?

Child: She probably bought it thinking about self-defense, but maybe she had another part of her brain that said, "Did I really have to buy it? It's dangerous and there are the kids in the house."

Dad: If the aunt purchases a gun and keeps it in her purse, how will the boy and girl feel about that when they go to visit her?

Child: Curious.

Dad: How is the mother feeling?

Child: I think that the mother might feel a little bit like, what's that word? Cautious.

Dad: Yeah, cautious. Has anything like this story ever happened to you?

Child: I've never had an experience with me and my friends with a gun but I've had an experience with a knife. My friend said, "Do you want to see the knife that my dad bought for us?" She was showing it to me.

Dad: What kind of knife was that?

Child: It was like one of those really sharp knives. It was in a case. But I was really scared about that because I was like thinking, "Oh boy. This girl and her brothers and friends know where the knife is. Stuff can happen."

Lessons Learned from This Sample Talk

In this talk the parent was surprised to hear that his daughter had had an incident with a knife that scared her. This is clearly a time to reinforce the message that whenever the child sees a weapon of any kind, even in a case, the parent wants to know about it. The parent can ask why the daughter didn't tell him about the knife incident, particularly since the daughter seemed to feel that it's more mature to keep quiet and let things blow over. The child seemed to understand the potential dangers of having a gun with children around. The parent might talk about safety procedures for people who have guns and have children living in or visiting the home.

8

Screening Out Problems

Talking about Violence on the Internet

One thousand thirty-eight young people ages thirteen to seventeen offered a snapshot of what some call Generation Y, a swath of adolescents so cybersavvy that 63 percent report using a computer at home, up from 45 percent in 1994, and 42 percent have E-mail addresses.—1999 New York Times/CBS News nationwide poll

My daughter was doing a school report on breast cancer and was looking for a web site and instead found a world of sites for men who love pictures of big-breasted women.
—Patrice, mother of two, Fairfax, Virginia

My fourth-grade son wanted to buy his friend a birthday present, and typed in "hot new toys and games" on the Internet—up comes something like "downunder sextoys.com, an Australian Internet supplier of mail order adult products." Not exactly what either of us had in mind.—Rachel, mother of one, Portland, Oregon

Microsoft's commercials for their company web site asked, "Where do you want to go today?" For millions of kids the answer is easy: to chat rooms and adult–only porno sites. Many parents voice their concern that raising Internet-safe children is a challenge. You may be thinking that it was hard enough raising kids to be careful with strangers they might meet in person—coming home from school or in the neighborhood. Now, when your kids go on-line they have access to literally millions of strangers. And like any public space, some of the people in the chat rooms are not the kinds of folks with whom you would want your child to spend time.

First, here's the good news about the Internet. When used appropriately, it's a tool for international commerce, a resource center, and an information trading post connecting people from around the world. It's revolutionizing business, education, and family life, making communication faster and more efficient.

Now the bad news. At the touch of a button, your daughter can enter chat rooms and talk with a thirty-two-year-old man pretending to be a twelve-year-old female peer. She could send a picture of herself to hundreds of strangers, along with her address, phone number, and the name of her school. Your son can enter sites containing as much sexually explicit material as the sleaziest adult bookstore. Anyone can create web sites that demean other people and incite violence against individuals or groups of people. Your kids can browse sites that promote the sale of weapons to minors. To complicate the matter, when asked how trustworthy the information and people on the Internet are, many children (and some adults) compare it to the library and say they see it as a place where all the information is true.

Preparing for the Talk

This talk about the Internet touches on many topics including personal boundaries; private versus public information; your family's values about sexually explicit images, videos, and web sites; and the risk of inciting violence. This is a necessary conversation, since your child is growing up with access to the Internet—whether at home, school, the library, or at friends' houses. In this talk you will let your child know that

- the Internet can be a great tool for learning and socializing, but has to be used thoughtfully and carefully.
- she can depend on you for help when encountering disturbing sites or people online.
- you have expectations about what kinds of personal information he can share online.
- there are family rules about using the Internet.

What You Can Expect from the Talk

After the talk your child will

- understand that the Internet can be a valuable tool for education, enrichment, commerce, and fun.
- understand that some sites are very well researched and truthful while others are filled with inaccuracies and outright lies.
- understand that chat rooms are filled with all kinds of people, not all of whom are who they say they are.
- understand the family rules about using the Internet and visiting adult-only sites, sites that encourage violence, or chat rooms.

The World of the Internet

The Internet can enrich children's lives in many ways. But it's a complex, unregulated environment in which kids need guidance and a code of behavior. In many ways, most parents already have some rules in place to help their children use the Internet. They are the same rules that apply to watching violence on TV, talking with strangers, using the phone, and visiting adult bookstores—all rolled into one. The Internet, like the TV, is filled with messages promoting violence and images of gratuitous violence to women, men, and children. The rules you have about TV viewing can be applied to the Internet. The Internet is filled with chat rooms where millions of strangers talk with one another, sharing all kinds of personal information and desires. This is where the rule about "talking with strangers" applies. If you have rules about what kinds of personal information your child can share with a stranger that she meets on the street or who calls her on the phone, these same rules can apply to "friends" she meets in a chat room.

Finally, you may have rules about your child buying or viewing sexually explicit magazines or videos. These rules can also apply to X-rated web sites that your child will find online.

Influence of the Media

TV programs and movies often show the Internet as a tool for average families, teachers, and business people as well as spies, action heroes, and villains. Science fiction stories let people enter the Internet to explore cyberland, where—to no one's surprise—male stars get to have virtual sex with the females of their dreams. There are cautionary films like *The Net,* which shows what happens when a corrupt computer company changes the identity of an honest woman—giving her a fake police record and canceling her credit cards. In general, the U.S. media's portrayal of the Internet is uncritical except for the few sick people who set out to rule the world by controlling the Internet. It is interesting to note that intelligence and access to information is often valued more than brute strength in the Internet age, allowing females with laptops to be just as powerful as men—often saving the day through quick keyboarding.

If you were thinking that the Internet might provide you and your child with a vacation from TV's incessant commercials, you are wrong. Companies use the Internet as another marketing tool to promote their advertising campaigns. Consumerism is highly promoted on the web, with tie-ins to TV commercials and print ads.

Pressure from Peers

The Internet is a fun place to go—for both children and adults. Your child and his friends will think so after visiting their first chat room and chatting with other kids. Chat rooms for kids and adults have taken off, and can become addictive. If you have visited chat rooms, you can see why they are so engaging. If you have not been in a chat room yet, get your child to help you navigate through one or go to your local library or computer store to give it a try.

My teenage daughter insists on having her full name in her online profile so that her friends can find her. This is something we continually fight over.—Karen, mother of two, West Linn, Oregon

It's been an eye opener, watching my normally shy son on the Internet. When he enters a chat room to talk with girls, he is anything but shy. In some ways I think it's good that he can experiment with being social on the Internet, but I wonder if he's really learning how to be bolder in real life.—Heather, mother of three, Jamestown, New York

Giving Your Child the Big Picture

Proportion of 18- to 24-year-olds who are online: 49%

Proportion of 50- to 64-year-olds who are: 21%

Proportion of those aged 65 and older who are: 6%

Proportion of U.S. households that are online: 30%

Proportion of the web-using population that has been online for 30 months or less: 80%

(Source: Harris Survey Unit, Baruch College, in the Public Perspective, *April/May 1998)*

Percent of American Schools reporting having Internet access in 1999: 90%

(Source: Technology in Education 1999, *Market Data Retrieval)*

In some ways, web surfers mirror U.S. society almost perfectly; women and men are represented in just about equal numbers, and the racial breakdown is a near-perfect reflection of society at large.

Clearly, both males and females enjoy the efficient and engaging qualities of the web, whether getting information for a school report, buying a new game, or chatting in a chat room. But there's one part of the web that is trafficked almost exclusively by males: the thousands of sites that promote the sale of sexually explicit magazines, pictures, and videos. While it would be impossible for a fourth-grade boy to visit an adult bookstore, the pornography can now come to him via the Internet. That's why talking about such sites with your child is important. Young people are being exposed to sexually explicit images at alarmingly early ages.

I never thought that I'd have to talk with my son about pornography while he was in elementary school but the Internet brings this adult stuff right into his bedroom. We get E-mails from sex shops all the time trying to sell X-rated magazines and videos. I don't know how they got my E-mail address. I'm not a prude, but there is no reason for kids to be exposed to this stuff.
—Donna, mother of one, Kansas City, Missouri

My daughter is online a lot. She says there is nothing else to do. She wants to find a boyfriend. I know that is her goal. But I can see lots of problems with the chat rooms. It's going to take a lot of talks and prohibiting the use of the computer behind closed doors for a while.
—Darcy, mother of one, Pine Ridge, South Dakota

Different Families: Different Values

There seem to be certain freedoms that people take when they enter chat rooms anonymously. Some people also feel free to post all kinds of unsubstantiated information on web sites without regard for accuracy or ethics. There are no "truth police" or fact checkers on the Internet. The following scenarios illustrate the kinds of messages your child may be receiving. Consider the following:

Some students at your child's school have designed their own web site. The site includes messages about individual students—saying some are stupid while others superior. The site says that certain students are "gonna get it."

Some parents might see this web site as acceptable—perhaps as merely "boys being boys." Others see it as threatening and intimidating. Some parents would ask school officials to support taking the site down.

■

A young girl goes online and is chatting in a room for teens. A person sends her a message asking for her picture and her name.

Some parents let their child go into teen chat rooms and don't mind her trading pictures or names, while other parents understand that teen chat rooms often have predatory adults in them pretending to be teens, as well as the occasional emotionally disturbed young person. Some parents don't want their child giving out pictures or any personal information online and have clear rules about such behavior.

■

A boy goes into an adults-only web site where there are sexually explicit pictures of women in scenes that suggest the threat of violence.

Some parents might see this as normal curiosity, comparing it to sneaking a peak at a Playboy centerfold when they were young. Other parents might find this material objectionable and block all such sites from their computer.

Last-minute Checkups before the Talk

When you were a child, the Internet as we know it did not exist. However, you probably had some family rules about buying X-rated magazines or sharing personal information with strangers—the very issues that child Internet use raises. Before you talk with your child, it helps to think about the following questions.

- When you were a child, did a parent ever tell you not to give your name, address, or phone number to strangers?
- Were you allowed to go into adult bookstores or to read X-rated magazines?
- Have you talked with your child about Internet use?
- Does he ever surf the Internet at home, at school, or at a friend's?
- Does he know what a chat room is? And if he entered one, would he know not to reveal his last name, address, or phone number?
- Does your child send pictures of herself to others across the Internet?
- Have you set limits on the amount of time he can spend online?
- Have you screened out X-rated web sites with the appropriate software?
- If your child were to find web sites advocating violence toward anyone, would he tell you about it?

If you have had any experience chatting with people online or visiting sites that you found disturbing, you might want to share them with your child. Many of us have a horror story about a single friend who "met" someone online, exchanged pictures, and met the person for coffee, only to find out that the person used a fake picture and appeared mentally unstable. The point of sharing some stories is to let your child know that people online are not always who they appear to be. Your child needs to hear that the Internet can be a wonderful place to learn and meet new people, but only if he follows certain safety guidelines.

What Are Your Family Rules?

Even if your child is not using the Internet at home, if she's past third grade she most likely has access at school or at a friend's house. Do you have family rules about Internet use? If not, this is a good time to think about them. The talk outlined in this chapter highlights the following situations:

- A girl talking in an Internet chat room
- A boy surfing the web
- A girl and boy discovering a web site promoting violence

Discussing these situations will give you an opportunity to discuss your family rules. What would you want your child to do in each situation? What are your expectations? Before the talk, think about what rules you want to communicate with your child. At the end of the talk, you will have the chance to review the rules with your child.

The Talk

Introduce the Talk

With five minutes of free time and your book in hand tell your child, "I need to talk with you about the Internet." Your child may be surprised that you have any interest in the web. Ask your child, "What do you know about the Internet?"

The response may range from "I don't know" or "I haven't used it yet" to "Do you want me to show you the best sites?"

For the child who has not yet surfed the web, you can describe it as a cross between a giant electronic library, a café where people chat, and a shopping mall. People use it to learn about the world, to do work, to meet other people, and to buy things. It's made up of sites that are maintained by all kinds of businesses, organizations, and people. Some sites are useful and some are not very good at all. It's similar to a TV in that some of the programs are fun and interesting while other programs are big commercials that only want to sell you useless stuff.

Review These Words

You may want to review these terms with your child. Reading them aloud is optional, depending on your child's age. If your child has been online, she most likely is familiar with the majority of these terms. The term "first amendment rights" may be new, but it is a very important one.

chat room: an area on the Internet where people type messages back and forth to one another.

First Amendment rights: the right to say almost anything you want about anything, even if it is hurtful or disrespectful. This applies to people, the media, and the Internet.

IM: abbreviation for Instant Messages, an internet feature that allows any two people to have a private, one-on-one, real-time correspondence, or "chat."

Internet: an international collection of computer files with millions of images and words.

LOL: abbreviation used in Internet chat rooms, meaning "laughing out loud"—one of many abbreviations in common use on the web.

network gaming: computer games on the Internet played by many people, often from all over the world, at the same time. Some of the games are very violent.

parental controls: software that can help people block out certain sites and words from the computer.

pic: stands for picture. It's common for people to scan a picture of themselves into the computer and then send it to people they talk to in a chat room.

profile: many times people using chat rooms have a profile of themselves that a viewer can access at the touch of a button. This profile can give any kind of personal information the person wants to share with the world (age, marital status, height, weight, interests, etc.).

screen name: the name you give yourself for your E-mail; also called a "handle."

trading pics: sending a picture of yourself to someone in return for his.

X-rated sites: sites that carry sexually explicit material.

Why Is Talking about Violence on the Internet Important?

Let your child tell you why talking about the Internet, and having rules about using it, might be important. Here are some reasons to consider:

- Talking about the Internet helps people identify potentially dangerous situations that may occur online.
- Talking about the Internet helps people understand that the

chat rooms are filled with all kinds of people, some good and some who are not who they appear to be.

- Talking about the Internet helps people know what to do if they are asked to visit sites that are sexually explicit or that promote violence

The Stories

In the next part of the talk, you'll be reading short stories to your child and discussing them together. You don't have to read all of the stories. Pick the ones that you think are appropriate for your child. The stories are very simple. Feel free to embellish them, adding details that you think might make the story more believable to your child.

The Story about the Girl in the Chat Room

This story offers a chance to discuss rules about Internet use.

"A girl is visiting a chat room and thinks she is chatting with a boy who has said he is her age. He asks for her name and phone number."

Ask these questions of your child:

- What is the girl thinking?
- What is the girl writing back to the boy?

Now that your child has completed this scenario, ask the following questions:

- Can the girl be certain that the boy is really who he says he is?
- Who else could the boy be?
- Why would anyone lie about himself in a chat room?

The person has sent a picture and it looks like a boy her age. Does that mean it really is a picture of the person she is chatting with?

- Should she send a picture of herself?
- Should she give out her phone number? Address? The name of the school she attends?
- Should she agree to talk with the person on the phone?
- Should she agree to meet the person? How might she feel about the idea of meeting a guy her age who seems to be kind and attractive?

Clarify Your Family's Values

Discuss these questions with your child as a way of sharing your values about the Internet. A number of potential responses from children are included to help you formulate your own responses.

Parent: How does someone know if the person she is talking with in a chat room is really who he says he is?
Child: If he sends a picture of himself.

Parent: How do you know that the picture he sends is really him?

Child: Why would he send a fake one?

Parent: If he sends a picture you find attractive, you might want to meet him.

The Story about the Boy and the Web Site

This story is an opportunity to discuss rules about Internet use and rules about reading, viewing and buying sexually explicit materials.

"A boy is online. He gets a message asking him to visit a fun new web site just by clicking on the word 'go.' He clicks it and finds himself at a site with pictures of nude men and women."

Ask these questions of your child:

- What is the boy thinking?
- What does he think his parents would think of him visiting this site with sexual and violent overtones?

Now that your child has completed this scenario, ask the following questions:

- Should he download the pictures?
- Should he tell his parents about the site?

Clarify Your Family's Values

Erotic and sexually explicit images have been around for thousands of years. Many people—mostly males—enjoy them. There is a range of erotic magazines and videos. Some are sensual and romantic, while others combine nudity with scenes of simulated violence. Parents should have family rules about buying such materials and having them in the home. And a discussion of the rules might include reasons why such images are not welcome in the house, how they represent males and females, and how respectful or disrespectful they are.

Discuss these questions with your child as a way of sharing your values about viewing sexually explicit images. A number of potential responses from children are included to help you formulate your own responses.

Parent: What are our family rules about sexually explicit images in this house?

Child: I don't know.

Parent: Well, let's talk about the rules we have for young people viewing sexually explicit material. It's the same whether it's a magazine, or a video, or online. (This is where you need to express your family's values.)

The Story about Violence Online

This story gives you an opportunity to discuss rules about Internet use and viewing potential threats of violence or intimidation.

"A boy and girl are visiting a site made

by some students from their school. The site talks about threatening students who don't fit in. It mentions several students by name and says that they should be 'blown away' because they 'don't belong in the school.' The boy and girl aren't sure if the site is serious or a joke."

Ask these questions of your child:

- What is the boy thinking?
- What is the girl thinking?
- What is the girl saying?
- What is the boy saying?

Now that your child has completed this scenario, ask the following questions:

- Should the boy and girl tell their parents about the site?
- What happens if they don't tell their parents about the site?
- What happens if they do tell their parents about the site?
- What if the boy and girl disagree on what to do?
- How can this site be harmful if it's meant only as joke?
- What would happen if the site encouraged people to hurt the students who didn't fit in?

Clarify Your Family's Values

Ask these questions to discuss your views on people who promote violence toward others.

Parent: "When a web site tells people it's okay to hurt other people, what can a person do?"

Child: "I don't know."

Parent: "If it's a student, a person can complain to the school and have the principal look into the situation."

Child: "How about if it's a grown-up who made the site?"

Parent: "If the site is asking people to hurt other people, then there may be a law against it. It depends on many things. But telling the police about the site is a good idea."

Parent: "If you see a site that asks people to hurt others, is it better to be an observer and just ignore it and not get involved?"

Child: "I don't know."

Parent: "One option is to ignore it. But if it's a schoolmate who wants to see other students or staff at your school get hurt, then the site may be a warning sign of actual violence to come. You never know."

The Bare Minimum: A Quick Quiz for Kids

Ask your child the following questions to assess her perception and knowledge of the Internet.

1. What is the best thing about the Internet?

2. What is the worst thing about the Internet?

3. What is an example of how someone could get into a potentially dangerous situation by using the Internet?
   Sample answers:
   - After giving out your phone number to someone in a chat room, you start getting frightening phone calls.

- After giving out your address to someone in a chat room, you get a visitor you don't want.
- After giving out your picture and school address to someone in a chat room, you are visited by someone you don't want to meet.
- You get unwanted or threatening messages from someone you met in a chat room until you block the unwanted e-mails.

Talk about Your Family Rules

What are our family rules about using the Internet?
Sample answers:
- Always tell me when you see sites in which there are messages about violence toward people.
- Never give out your password, last name, phone number, address, the name of your school, or our family income when talking with people in chat rooms.
- Always tell me if you get invitations to visit sexually explicit sites. And please don't download pictures that are sexually explicit.
- Don't ever give out a credit card number or your photo online without my permission.

After the Talk

A Moment to Reflect

Take a moment to reflect on the talk you just had with your child. You have many options when it comes to helping your child navigate the Internet safely. How do you feel about your computer now?

- Did your child share any information that surprised you?
- Do you have a new interest in blocking certain adult sites? The computer is like the TV. It contains programming that needs screening which can come only from the parent.
- Does your child understand the serious consequences of sharing personal information over the Internet?
- Do you feel that you can trust your child to refrain from using Internet chat rooms to meet people you might not approve of? Are you satisfied that everything is under control?
- How much of the time were you listening to your child?

Warning Signs

If your child is spending hours online in chat rooms, this may indicate a problem. It's normal to find the novelty of chat rooms pleasurable. But cyberspace chat rooms are best visited in moderation. Staring at a computer screen for hours is physically unhealthy. Compulsively visiting chat rooms to meet people is not a substitute for learning how to be social in the real world. Chat rooms can become addictive. This is true for adults and young people alike. If your child refuses to limit his time online you may want to consider getting outside help, or restricting the use of the computer.

Finding Help

The best place to look for help is often with family and friends—especially those who have computers and kids. If they have been through this and have set up their own family rules about Internet use, they may be able to provide valuable insight. If your child is obsessed with using the Internet for chatting and visiting adults-only sites, you might ask the school counselor for advice and referrals.

Success Stories

Yes, you did it! Talk number eight is over. Depending on whether your child is online or not, and how curious he is about cyberspace, this talk may or may not have been an easy one. We live in a new electronic culture with benefits and drawbacks for kids with computers and modems. An attorney in Seattle, Washington, used the talk to explain issues of copyright and intellectual property to his daughter; she found it fascinating. One mom in Denver, Colorado, realized her daughter was sending out her full name, school, and picture over the Internet—the result of the talk wasn't a fight but a heartfelt conversation about safety. (The daughter is much more careful now.) Lots of parents are finding that their kids are willing to be more careful, but that up until this talk, they hadn't given online safety much thought. But the biggest success is showing your child that you care enough to listen.

Sample Talks
Between Parents and Children

If you are wondering how a talk based on this chapter might really sound, take a look at the following excerpts from real family talks.

Discussing the Story about the Girl in the Chat Room

Participants: a mother and her eighth-grade daughter.

Mom: A girl is visiting a chat room and thinks she is chatting with a boy who says he is her age. He asks her for her name and phone number. What is the girl thinking?

Child: She's probably deciding whether she wants to tell the boy her name and phone number.

Mom: What is the girl typing?

Child: If I was her, I'd write a fake name and not give my number.

Mom: Can the girl be certain that the boy is really who he says he is?

Child: No, because you're only typing on the Internet and you have no proof of who it is.

Mom: Who else could the boy be?

Child: The boy could be some kind of sicko who likes to play with kids' minds or try to get them to go someplace where he could actually end up hurting them.

Mom: Why would anyone lie about themselves in a chat room?

Child: To get something.

Mom: The person has sent a picture and it looks like a boy her age. Does that mean it really is a picture of the person she is chatting with?

Child: No, because you can download pictures and send them to people on the Internet.

Mom: Should she send a picture of herself?

Child: No, because then if he does see her, he could do something to her. If she does want to send a picture, she should just get one off the Internet and send it to him.

Mom: Should she give out her phone number?

Child: No, because that's a way of contacting her. If he did call, he might get her address and come to her house.

Mom: Should she give out her address or the name of the school she goes to?

Child: Absolutely not, because that's just another way to get kidnapped or have something else bad happen to her.

Mom: Should she agree to talk with the person on the phone?

Child: No, because nothing good could happen in talking to a stranger.

Mom: Should she agree to meet with the person?

Child: No, because you never know what's going to happen if you meet a stranger.

Lessons Learned from This Sample Talk

The mother was reassured that her daughter understood the rules about giving out personal information over the Internet. Further talks could probe what might happen if she developed a "relationship" over time with an attractive peer in a chat room. Might she be tempted to share a phone number or would she call the person? The parent might ask: How does it feel to make a new "friend" online?

Discussing the Story about Violence Online

Participants: a mother and a sixth-grade son of a good friend of hers. The child's mom was happy to have another parent who was Internet-savvy talk with her son.

Adult: A boy and girl are visiting a site made by some students from their school. The site talks about threatening students who don't fit in. It mentions several students by first name and says that they should be "blown away" because they "don't belong in the school." The boy and girl aren't sure if the site is a joke or serious. What are they thinking?

Child: Are these guys crazy? Is this real? (short laughs) I mean, could this really happen?

Adult: That's what he's thinking when he sees the site?

Child: Yeah. He's thinking, "Is this me? Do I fit in? Am I doing the right thing? Am I cool?"

Adult: So he's trying to figure out if his name would be on the list?

Child: Uh-huh.

Adult: The girl sitting next to him is also looking at the site. What is she thinking?

Child: Probably the same thing. Do I fit in? What have I done wrong?

Adult: Who do you think made up the site?

Child: Probably someone older who's more popular in the school and they get a whole lot more attention.

Adult: What are the boy and girl saying to each other as they are looking at this site?

Child: I think they might be shocked. Maybe they are saying, "What do you think this is? Is it a joke? What should we do? Who should we tell?" Stuff like that.

Adult: Should the boy and girl tell their parents about the site?

Child: Yes. Probably.

Adult: What happens if they do not tell their parents about the site?

Child: I don't know. Trouble I guess.

Adult: What happens if they do tell their parents about the site?

Child: I think they'd be pretty happy that the kids told them about what they found. They wouldn't like the site.

Adult: What do you think the parents will do once their kids tell them about the site?

Child: I think they'll probably call the principal or somebody in charge that knows the kids or whoever made the site.

Adult: How can this site be harmful, even if it is only a joke?

Child: Well some people might think, "Oh, I don't fit in," and feel bad or scared.

Adult: What would happen if the site asked people to hurt the students that didn't fit in?

Child: I think that would be pretty bad. I'd be scared. I'd be sad if I didn't fit in and I would probably want to fit in and change the way I do things, who I sit with at lunch, the way I talk, the way I dress, stuff like that.

Adult: Okay, the site said to stay away from a particular person, even if he was a casual friend, then you might stop talking to that person just because the site said, "This guy's a geek" and "No one should sit next to him anymore."

Child: I don't know. If it was a joke I would go up to that kid and maybe say something or I'd stay with the geeky kid, if he was my casual friend.

Adult: What might happen if you told someone about the site and the person who made the site got in a lot of trouble? Do you think that person might come back to harm you?

Child: They might threaten you or come back and harm you but I wouldn't be scared. I would just tell somebody to watch my back.

Adult: Have you ever seen a site like this?

Child: No. I just go to Nintendo cheat sites and song lyrics sites and stuff for school.

Lessons Learned from This Sample Talk

This talk is an excellent example of how a parent's trusted friend can have a successful talk with a child. The adult and child discussed some ways to deal with potentially harmful and hurtful web sites. Further talks could explore peer group pressure, the need to fit in, and what the phrase "have somebody watch my back" means. The adult might ask: How does it feel to not fit in? Are there kids you know who don't seem to fit in? How are these kids treated?

9

Finding Good Friends

Talking about Healthy Relationships

*I grew up in a very abusive family and I know that the one thing
that got me through it all, up to this day, was my friendships.*
—Ray, father of two, Jamestown, New York

*People know they are in a healthy, mature friendship when they are
certain that they are unconditionally loved. They are confident about
their own ability to love and that the other person recognizes and
responds to that love. Healthy friendships must include conflict
management skills, self-awareness and emotional independence. We
cannot look to the other person to fill our personal voids.*
—April Roseman, psychotherapist, Seattle, Washington

*I know people who say they have dozens of friends—all people I
would call acquaintances. It makes me wonder what people consider
a friend.*—Vanessa, mother of three, Memphis, Tennessee

Having friendships and a support group can go a long way in
keeping your child safe from a lot of violent people. In this
chapter we want to take a very positive approach and focus on the
kinds of relationships that will make your child's life richer,
stronger, and safer.

A core belief expressed in this book is that people have the power to make choices about their behaviors. Your child has some choices about what kinds of people he spends time with. Friendships can play a big part in your child's life, and it's the quality of these relationships that is the focus of this chapter. We also will look at what you can do to monitor the quality of your child's friendships.

The talk in this chapter will focus on how your child learns what it takes to have a friend and to be a friend. It will give you an opportunity to talk about the difference between buddies or girlfriends who "hang out" and intimate friends who can discuss problems and talk about how they are feeling. This talk will especially be helpful for boys who tend to be good at "doing things" but unskilled at communicating feelings. This talk can also help children evaluate their relationships to see if they are getting what they need and being treated with the respect they deserve.

Preparing for the Talk

On a practical level, having friendships provides a support group that can keep a child safe from aggressive peers and adults. This talk, like all the talks, is not meant to provide you with a psychological assessment of your child, but it is designed to give you the tools to better understand your child's attitudes and social skills. This talk also will give you the chance to talk about what friendship means to you and the many kinds of friendships that can exist. It also can give you a better picture of the kinds of people your child is spending time with and is being influenced by.

In this talk you will help your child understand that

- friendships can play a very important part in a person's life.
- having a circle of friends can make a person feel safer and less vulnerable to violence.
- there are many types of friendships, from casual acquaintances to intimate friends.
- there are family rules about what one does when spending time with friends.

What You Can Expect from This Talk

After the talk your child will be able to

- define "friendship" and describe the different types of friendships.
- differentiate between casual buddies or acquaintances and intimate friendships.
- understand how friendships can offer support during potentially difficult times.
- understand how peer pressure from friends can affect our behavior.
- know where to get help when having problems with friends or making friends.

What Is Friendship?

The word "friend" means different things to different people. In day care or elementary school, we aren't the most discerning about whom we spend time with. Most of us are just happy to have someone to play with as long as they don't hit us. As we grow more mature, we take on a unique personality and begin to understand that there are different kinds of people with their own ways of seeing the world. We have more of a give-and-take approach to friendship that even may include what some call "fair weather friends." Progressing through grade school, we look for more intimacy and support. We are willing to endure conflict for the sake of friendship, and sometimes experience possessiveness and jealousy. Eventually, if all goes well, by the time we are ready for middle school, we have developed a more in-depth perspective. We begin to realize that we are interdependent with our friends, and we gradually accept others' needs to have relationships with other people.

When I was in school, having different friendships gave me the opportunity to experiment and try out different ways of talking. With some friends I was shy and with others more bold.
—Jen, mother of three, Seattle, Washington

My older sister was always popular, but finding friendships was not so easy for me. There was always competition—sometimes even conflict—when I tried to develop new friends that my sister thought were "hers." Things settled down once I got into high school.
—Drew, mother of two, Kansas City, Missouri

As a kid I felt like I got through life day to day. My house was not a place I wanted to be for a lot of good reasons. Having friends was a necessity and made all the difference in the world.
—Doug, father of three, Memphis, Tennessee

I don't think my sons know what real friendship is. They are good at playing sports or electronic games with their male friends, but I don't see them really talking about anything of importance. Their circle of friends changes often, and it's almost as though the guys are inter-changeable. It doesn't really matter who is in the group as long as there is a group to play with.—Debra, mother of four, Yakima, Washington

Families and Friendships

We first learn to socialize from our family. In large families, we learn about friendships from watching our parents, grandparents, and other adults, as well as relating to our siblings or other young relatives. In small families we may have only one parent to observe until we enter day care or school. Some families encourage their kids to develop friendships, while others prefer a close-knit or controlled home situation where people outside the family are not usually invited in.

For the child growing up in a family where threats of violence are commonplace, visiting a friend's home and watching her friend's parents relating to each other may be the first time she sees healthy adult relationships. For the child with a violent parent, ob-serving and relating to an even-tempered adult is an important role-modeling experience. Some parents never have friends come visit. Others have a parent with friends who sit and talk about life over a cup of coffee. For some parents, their spouse represents his or her only friend. Regardless of what kind of friendships your parents have, they serve as role models that give you messages about the role of friendships.

Parents often give messages about friends versus family. Some of us were told that we don't tell anybody about certain experiences or discuss certain topics. The phrase "keep it in the family" sug-gests that friends can't be trusted with certain kinds of information. In some cases, the secrets that our family members told us to keep from friends were precisely the kinds of information and experiences that should be shared with a good friend.

I was sexually abused by my older brother for years, and my parents would not believe me when I told them. It wasn't until I told my girlfriends in high school that I felt supported. If I hadn't had had those friends, I don't think I would have made it.
—Phyllis, Seattle, Washington

I have two types of family members. Some are what I call blood family and others I call my chosen family. My chosen family members are the ones who nurture me, and I make a point to see them. But my blood family is still a part of my life that I take in very small doses.
—Sandy, Philadelphia, Pennsylvania

A lot of families have secrets. And it must be a terrible burden on the child. My son has a schoolmate whose father was in jail. He's now out of jail, living in another state. It's never spoken about. I'm sure the child would be horrified if her classmates knew.
—Trish, mother of two, San Antonio, Texas

Influence of the Media

Hollywood produces comedies that feature males described as "friends" who actually may act more like buddies, casual acquaintances, or childish pals. Adults in sitcoms, for the sake of humorous antics, are scripted to act more like seventh graders than mature adults. Soap operas rarely show loyalty between friends since their plots, dependent on drama, almost demand that "friends" betray each other. We see lots of buddy films, where guys play poker, get drunk, or try to seduce the same woman, but rarely show emotion or caring.

Finding good role models in media takes a lot of time and energy. Some cable stations cater more to women, producing shows that portray intimacy, maturity, or sharing of serious problems between friends. TV programs, video, or films that illustrate deep friendships do exist but are sandwiched between a multitude of stories filled with action or slapstick. If you want to show your child how to make friends and the qualities that make a friendship work, you most likely will have to do some research in your local video rental store. And you'll want to watch these programs with your child and discuss the themes of the movies together. You also can introduce books to younger children that illustrate strong friendships. Your local librarian or bookseller can make some age-appropriate recommendations.

When my daughters were in elementary school, I tried to read to them each night after they got in bed. Good books can provide role models and illustrate the value of friendship better than TV ever can.
—Karen, mother of two, Portland, Oregon

What Do You Look for in a Friend?

Think about your childhood for a moment.

- What did you find attractive about other people?
- What was it about other young people that drew you to them? Was it their personality, sense of humor, and intelligence? Was it their physical appearance?

- How important was the way they were dressed and the neigh-borhood they lived in?

Now that you are an adult, what do you look for in friends?

- How have your views on friendship changed over the years?
- Do you look for people who share your values and beliefs?
- What are the most important qualities a friend must have now?
- What qualities does your child look for in a friend?

What Are Friendship Skills?

How does your child make friends? It's a skill that one develops over time and with experience. We don't receive a handbook called "How to Make Friends," but if there were one it might con-tain the following questions to help you take stock of your skills in relationship building. This may sound like common sense, but you might consider posing these questions to your child as part of your talk about healthy relationships.

When you spot someone who seems like a good person, do you know how to introduce yourself? How do you develop rela-tionships with people who seem like they could become close friends? How do you spot people who you think won't make good friends?

Once you have a friend, how do you nurture the relationship in a way that makes both people feel good? How do you keep from getting stuck with friendships that are not healthy? How do you end a friendship that makes you uncomfortable or unhappy? Do you think that males and females have different ideas about friend-ship and look for different qualities in a friend?

Quotable Parents

When my daughter was in fifth grade, her best friend moved away. She said she didn't want to go to school anymore because she had no friends. We talked about some girls in her class that she might like to be friends with and how to approach them. Within two weeks, she had two new "best friends."—Karen, mother of two, Portland, Oregon

I didn't really have friends in middle school, and it was a very stressful time. I related more to adults than kids my own age. I learned very quickly that if I didn't find some friends in high school I would always be vulnerable to the bigger guys. I was small for my age. It took me two years, but by my junior year I managed to create a very solid network of friends.—Dennis, father of two, Seattle, Washington

What I looked for in a friend in high school is not the same as what I look for now. Sure, the basics are the same—common interests, having fun together, and a feeling of kinship. But now I look for deeper things, like shared values and commitments to important issues.
—Beatrice, mother of three, Denver, Colorado

If I was in the hospital would they come visit? If I lost my apartment would they offer me a couch to sleep on? If I was having a crisis of some sort would they be there for me? These are the questions I ponder when I think about who is a friend. Friends are committed. Acquaintances are people to just do things with. When I was young everyone was a friend, or so I thought. I didn't really have any criteria for friends. Now I do. And I have gone from a guy with lots of acquaintances to someone with a small circle of special friends. It makes life easier and more satisfying.—Andrew, father of two, New York City

Different Families: Different Values

Everyone interprets behavior in his or her own way. Here are some behaviors that may be experienced differently depending on a person's background:

A boy and his friend are walking down the hall at school. An older student comes up and tries to start a fight with one of the boys, and his friend stands by and says nothing.

Some parents call this "letting people stand up for themselves." Others might say that a friend is someone who stands up for his friends. What do you think?

■

A girl is sitting with a group of her friends. She turns to two of the girls and invites them to her birthday party. She turns to a third girl and says, "Sorry, but my mom said I can only invite two friends over."

Some parents would say that this is normal behavior for girls. Others would say the girl should not be inviting some friends and excluding others so callously—if she can invite only two of her three friends, then she should invite the two in private and speak with the third friend separately. What do you think?

■

Two girls have plans to go to a movie on Friday night. Two hours before the movie, one of the girls calls the other to say that she just got a date with a guy she likes and is going to go out with him instead of going to the movies with her.

Some parents would say that this happens all the time and friends understand. Others might say that dumping a friend for a date is not very thoughtful, because a commitment to do something with a friend should be kept. What do you think?

The situations above illustrate the way people treat others who they call friends. Some of the behaviors may not be what you believe are appropriate ways to treat friends. What's important is to talk to your child about the qualities your child should look for in a friendship.

Last-minute Checkups before the Talk

Before you talk with your child, try to remember what your parents taught you about friendship when you were growing up.

- Did a parent ever talk to you about the importance of friendships?
- Did they tell you to stand up for your friends?
- Did they encourage you to bring your friends home?
- Did your parents have good friends of their own?

As a parent, what are you teaching your child about friendship?

- Do you encourage her to bring her friends home?
- How welcome do you make your child's friends feel?
- Do you talk to your child about ways to find new friends?
- Do you have your own friends over to the house?

Do you have any stories you can share with your child about friendships, how you made friends, or how they helped you out of potentially violent situations? For example:

- The time a friend defended you when a bully was threatening you
- The time you befriended someone
- The time you felt betrayed by a friend

Sharing your stories lets your child know how you feel about friendships and what they meant to you when you were growing up.

What Are Your Family Rules?

Do you have family rules about friendships and relationships? If not, this is a good time to think about them. This talk highlights the following situations:

- Two friends (boys) talking
- Two friends (girls) talking
- Two friends (a boy and girl) talking
- A group of friends (boys) threatening another boy
- A group of friends (girls) threatening another girl

The idea is to talk about what kinds of behaviors your child expects of friends. But the stories and questions are open-ended, allowing your child to reflect on a range of topics including the things friends do together, peer pressure, and any other problems or concerns. Depending on your child, the talk could even include issues of alcohol and drug use and sexual relationships. Discussing these situations will give you an opportunity to share your family rules about friendships and acceptable behavior.

The Talk

Introduce the Talk

If your child is expecting some doom or gloom, consider beginning by saying something like, "How are your friends?"

Expect your child to offer either an eager "Let me tell you . . ." or the opposite, "Why do you want to know?"

You could say, "I'm reading a chapter on friendships and I've got some questions for you. What makes a person a good friend?"

Your child may offer the following traits: someone who is nice, friendly, funny, good at sports, popular, likes to do stuff, or has good games. You can offer the following additional traits: loyal, thoughtful, caring, honest, trustworthy, ethical, fair, respectful, and a good sense of humor.

Review These Words

Please review the terms in this section. Discussing all the terms with your child is optional. You know which are appropriate for your child's age and maturity level. More than likely, even the youngest children have heard these words on TV.

acquaintance: a person you know a little, but not very well

buddy: a term used to describe a friend or a casual acquaintance

caring: concerned, thoughtful

ethical: having a system of morals, standards for how to treat people

honest: truthful

loyal: faithful to friends, a cause, or country

respectful: to think highly of and show concern for someone
thoughtful: considerate of others' feelings
trustworthy: reliable, to be trusted

Why Is Talking about Friendship Important?

Ask your child whether she thinks talking about friendship is important. Here are some reasons you might want to offer:

- Talking about friendship means learning to find and make good friends.
- Talking about friendship means learning to see how having good friends makes life easier.
- Having friends sometimes means feeling pressure from them to do things that are against our family rules, and I'd like to talk with you about how to deal with that pressure.
- Talking about friendship means clarifying family rules about friends.

The Stories

In the next part of the talk, you'll be reading short stories to your child and discussing them together. You don't have to read all of the stories. Pick the ones that you think are appropriate for your child. The stories are very simple. Feel free to embellish them, adding details that you think might make the story more believable to your child.

The first three stories are similar, but have different players: The first has two boys, the second, two girls, and the third, a boy and a girl. You can use one or all three to start a conversation about friendships. You may find it interesting to compare and contrast the way friendships between boys and girls are viewed by your child. These stories may seem redundant at first glance. But consider using them to focus on the different dynamics between males and females. If you are talking with your son, you can help him get a better understanding of how girls think and communicate. The opposite is true if you are talking with your daughter—you might let her in on how boys communicate with one another. Much has been written about how differently males and females communicate. The third story about the boy and girl gives you an opportunity to address these differences in communication styles with your child.

In addition to addressing how boys and girls communicate, the last two stories focus on how groups of boys and groups of girls might react to rude or cruel behavior from their friends.

The Story about Two Guys

This story is an opportunity to talk about what friends do with one another, what they talk about, and how they deal with peer pressure.

"Two boys have been friends for years. They are going somewhere for the afternoon." (You can decide where they are going.)

Ask these questions of your child:

• Where are they going?

- What are the boys saying?
- What are the boys thinking?

Now that your child has completed this scenario, ask the following questions:

- What kinds of things do guys talk about?
- How are these things different from what girls talk about?
- Are they both happy about where they are going?
- What would happen if one friend wanted to go somewhere or do something that the other friend knew was against his family rules? (For example, throw eggs at a car, shoplift, break into a home, drink beer, or watch a fight.)
- Have you ever been in a situation like this? If so, how did you feel? What did you do?

The Story about Two Girls

This story gives you a chance to talk about what friends do with one another, what they talk about, and how they deal with peer pressure.

"Two girls have been friends for years. They are going somewhere for the afternoon." (You can decide where they are going.)

Ask these questions of your child:

- Where are they going?

- What are the girls saying?
- What are the girls thinking?

Now that your child has completed this scenario, ask the following questions:

- What kinds of things do girls talk about?
- How are these things different from what boys talk about?
- Are they both happy about where they are going?
- What would happen if one friend wanted to go somewhere or do something that the other friend knew was against her family rules? (For example, smoke cigarettes, shoplift, go out with some older guys, or drink alcohol.)
- Have you ever been in a situation like this? If so, how did you feel? What did you do?

The Story about a Boy and a Girl

This story gives you an opportunity to talk about what friends do with one another, what they talk about, and how they handle peer pressure.

"A boy and a girl have been good friends for years. They are going somewhere for the afternoon." (You can decide where they are going.)

Ask these questions of your child:

- Where are they going?

- What is the girl saying?
- What is the boy saying?
- What is the girl thinking?
- What is the boy thinking?

Now that your child has completed this scenario, ask the following questions:

- What do boys and girls usually talk about?
- How are these things different from what boys talk about together?
- How are these things different from what girls talk about together?
- Are they both happy about where they are going?
- What would happen if one friend wanted to go somewhere or do something that the other friend knew was against the family rules? (For example, go to a party where people will be drinking, stay out late and break curfew, or get a tattoo.)
- Have you ever been in a situation like this? If so, how did you feel? What did you do?

The Story about Boys Who Threaten

This story gives you a chance to talk about what kinds of behaviors we accept from our friends. You will have an opportunity to compare and contrast how males and females behave using the following two stories.

"A guy is with a group of his

friends. One of his friends spots another student and calls out a cruel name, then knocks him in the head, as they are walking into school."

Ask these questions of your child:

- What did the friend call out?
- What does the guy who is watching think of his friend's behavior?
- Why did he the name-caller hit the other boy? What was he thinking?

Now that your child has completed this scenario, ask the following questions:

- What is the guy who was hit feeling?
- Why would someone want to spend time with a person who is rude or cruel to others?
- How can a person find friends who aren't cruel to others?
- What might happen if the guy told his friend that he didn't like to see people being called names or threatened?
- Have you ever been in a situation like this? If so, how did you feel? What did you do?

The Story about Girls Who Threaten

This story is about what kinds of behaviors we accept from our friends.

"A girl is with a group of her friends. One of her friends spots another student and calls out a cruel name and pushes her as they are walking into school."

Ask these questions of your child:

- What did the friend call out?
- What does the girl who is watching think of her friend's behavior?
- Why did the girl push the other student? What was she thinking?

Now that your child has completed this scenario, ask the following questions:

- What is the girl who was pushed feeling?
- Why would someone want to spend time with a person who is cruel to others?
- How can a person find friends who aren't cruel to others?
- What might happen if the girl told her friend that she didn't like to see people being called names or threatened?
- Have you ever been in a situation like this? If so, how did you feel? What did you do?

Clarify Your Family's Values

Discuss these questions with your child as a way of sharing your values about friendship. We have included a number of potential responses from children to help you formulate your own responses.

Ask your child: "When a person has a friend who does cruel things to others (name-calling, starting fights, etc.), what kind of a friend are they?"

Child response #1: A good one if they don't call me names.

Parent: It depends on the situation. Sometimes a friend has a bad day and does something mean. But if a friend is constantly cruel then there is a problem. We have a family rule about spending time with people who threaten others. And often calling people rude or cruel names is viewed as threatening others.

Child response #2: If you want me to give up every friend who calls people names then I won't have any friends.

Parent: Finding friends who are good people can take time. I know there is competition to find friends. And I know that having a group of friends at school can help you get through the day. There are people at your school who feel good about themselves and don't feel the need to threaten others. I'd like to see you spend some time making friends with those kinds of people. You may find you have more fun with kids like that.

The Bare Minimum: A Quick Quiz for Kids

Ask your child the following questions to assess her knowledge and perceptions of friendship.

1. Can you give me one example of how a person might show friendship?
   Sample answers:

- If a bully wants to beat up a student and that student's friend comes forward to break it up.
- A friend can invite his friend over to dinner and a movie with his family.
- A friend can talk about her or his feelings.
- A friend shows respect.

2. How does having friends make life safer?
   Sample answers:
- People with friends don't get picked on as much.
- People with friends have support at school and in the neighborhood.
- People with friends can feel more confident.
- People with friends feel less lonely and have someone to talk to about their frustrations.

3. What is an example of a friend asking you to do something that is not safe or thoughtful?
   Sample answers:
- A friend wants you to join him to go throw eggs at some houses and knock over some mailboxes.
- A friend wants you to help him make a web site that says rude, disrespectful, or cruel things about people.
- A friend makes fun of other people and expects you to support her.

I had a friend who invited me over to a slumber party. She said her parents would be there. When I got there her mom was gone and only an older brother and other older guys were there. They were drinking beer and watching X-rated videos. I was a little scared.
—Lisa, mother of one, Seattle, Washington

Talk about Your Family Rules

This is an opportunity to review your family rules. Ask your child the following question:

What are our family rules about friends?
Sample answers:

- Before you visit a friend's home, I want to meet the friend
- If a friend is violent in any way, I want to hear about it
- When you want to visit a friend's home, I need the friend's phone number because I might want to speak with one of his parents
- When your friends are threatened, come to their defense as long as it does not put you at risk of harm, or escalate a violent situation

After the Talk

Some parents are surprised by how much kids observe other cliques, groups, and gangs. Others see how cliques and groups in school have not changed much. Your goal is to help your child understand that she can make choices about the kinds of friends she has and the kinds of friend she is.

A Moment to Reflect

Take a moment to reflect on the talk you just had with your child. How do you feel about it?

- What surprised you about your child's view of friendship?
- Do you think she has good friends? Think about whether your

child has the ability to be a good friend, and how you might help nurture those friendship skills.
- How much of the time were you listening to your child?

Warning Signs

The talks may reveal potential problems that your child is facing. Is your child feeling isolated and alienated from friends? Is he someone who has only superficial relationships? We all go through periods of isolation. Has your child been in an isolated phase for what seems to be a very long time? Review the following warning signs to look for long-term situations.

- He doesn't appear to care if he has friends or not.
- She doesn't see anything wrong with treating friends badly or rudely.
- He doesn't see anything wrong with his friends threatening others.
- She doesn't want you to meet her friends.
- He thinks friends who talk about their feelings are weak.
- She shares some problems in the course of the talk that sound like they could be serious.

Trust your instincts on how your child is doing. When you meet your child's friends, do they appear well adjusted and well mannered? Have you spoken to the parents of your child's friends? Do they ever call you when their child is spending time at your home? Likewise, do you call your child's friends' parents in these situations?

Finding Help

This talk may reveal a number of issues. Your child may have hinted at having problems either making or keeping friends. Or he may have made up some serious "problems" for the characters in the stories. While presented as fantasy, the situations may indeed be based on real situations in your child's life. If needed, support and help for your child is available. Your child's school will have resources, and your family and friends may have helpful insights.

Success Stories

You have made it through talk number nine. One more to go! This talk about friendship has held a lot of surprises for parents. A shy child won't necessarily open up about how he feels. And the 15-year-old social butterfly isn't always aware of the power of her friendships. These talks are giving the parents the chance to discuss both the quantity and quality of their kids' friendships. You may not like your son's best friend or your daughter's boyfriend as much as you or they might want. But when parents and children sit down to talk, the success isn't that they agree on everything. The success is that they sit down together.

Sample Talks

Between Parents and Children

If you are wondering how a talk based on this chapter might really sound, take a look at the following excerpts from real family talks.

Discussing the Story about a Boy and a Girl

Participants: a mother and her eighth-grade son.

Mom: This boy and girl have been friends for years, like you and Dana. They are going somewhere. Where do you want to have them going?

Child: A movie.

Mom: Are they happy about where they are going?

Child: If it's a movie they both want to see.

Mom: What would happen if one friend wanted to go somewhere or do something that the other friend knew was against the family rules? Like one friend said, let's go throw eggs at a car, break into a house, drink some beer, something like that.

Child: I don't know. The kid would say "no."

Mom: Have you ever been with a friend who wanted you to do something that you felt would get you into trouble?

Child: Probably, yes.

Mom: Okay, so what would happen if you were in a situation like this, that someone wanted to do something that you didn't? What would you do to get out of it or would you just do what your friend wants to do?

Child: I'd say no.

Mom: And do what? Just walk away or try to convince them not to do it?

Child: I'd just say, "I'm not going to."

Mom: Has this happened to you?

Child: I thought I just said that. Yes.

Mom: And what happened in that situation? Did the person do what they said they were going to do or did they not do it?

Child: No.

Mom: So you were a good influence on your friend?

Child: I guess.

Mom: It sounds to me like you were. Your good judgment saved your friend from getting in trouble. Don't you think so?

Child: Yes.

Lessons Learned from This Sample Talk

In this talk, the mother reinforced her son's decision not to go along with a friend who wanted to break the family rules. The mother pointed out that her son was a good friend by doing so. Future talks could probe what happens when one feels peer pressure to conform, have some "fun" with friends, and break, bend, or test the rules just a bit. The parent might ask: How do you feel telling your friends no?

Discussing the Story about Boys Who Threaten

Participants: a mother and her fifth-grade son.

Mom: A guy is with his group of buddies. One of his friends calls a student passing in the hall a cruel name. What is the guy who is watching thinking?

Child: "Why'd he call that guy a name?"

Mom: What is the guy who is name-calling thinking?

Child: "Ha ha."

Mom: What is the guy who is being called a name thinking?

Child: "Why'd you call me that, man?"

Mom: So he's defending himself?

Child: Yeah.

Mom: Why would someone want to spend time with a person who is cruel to others?

Child: Well if they seemed nice, like at first.

Mom: And you don't really know how cruel they are?

Child: Looks can be deceiving.

Mom: Do you have a friend who says cruel things about other people?

Child: No. I don't have any friends like that but I know about five people who do that.

Mom: How about your friends next door. How about when the older brother calls the younger brother a bad name? Do you stand up for the younger brother and say, "Hey, stop calling your brother that."

Child: Well, the younger brother doesn't really care because it's an everyday thing for him.

Mom: So you don't stand up for him?

Child: If he started to care, I would.

Mom: Have you been in any other situations where you told people to stop calling other people names?

Child: Well, people call each other "stupid."

Mom: That's cruel isn't it?

Child: Well, most people do that.

Mom: So that's an acceptable name to call people?

Child: No, and I tell them to stop.

Lessons Learned from This Sample Talk

In this talk, the mother and son were able to talk about the role of the observer when a friend was calling someone cruel names.

Although it can be difficult to stop a friend from hurting others without putting the friendship at risk, the mother tried to help her son understand that friends who are cruel may not be worth keeping. Sometimes when a child has only one friend it's not easy to give them up. People might prefer to have one cruel friend than be friendless. The son seems to have a sense of justice, and stops people from calling others "stupid." It's a good quality and can be reinforced in future talks. The parent might ask: How do you feel when you are called names? How do you feel when you hear others being called names?

Rules to Live By

Talking about Your Family's Beliefs

I like to talk about virtues with my kids. Tolerance, forgiveness, respect, tact, kindness, and gentleness are my favorites.
—June, mother of three, Boise, Idaho

I don't remember a time when I sat with my parents talking about their beliefs. There was no official talk. It was all unspoken and I suppose I learned from watching how they lived, rather than from what they said.—Brandon, father of two, Jamestown, New York

How do parents think their kids will learn their values if not through communication with their parents? Sometimes kids can pick up their family's values just by observing—but oftentimes kids misinterpret what they see. It's so important that parents tell their kids exactly what is important to them, and hear straight from their child what they are feeling and thinking.
—Pepper Schwartz, Ph.D., University of Washington

In developing parent involvement programs we have found some interesting views on teaching about character. If you ask teachers, they will say that it's really the job of the parents to do that. Some parents say that they think it's a good idea for schools to teach it. Of course, if you ask kids how they learn how people are supposed to treat one another in healthy relationships, they often mention TV. Now that is a scary thought.
—Susan Durón, Ph.D., consultant, Denver, Colorado

*Parents communicate their values and beliefs to their young children
every moment of every day, through words and actions—mostly
through behaviors. If a parent believes in nonviolence, this must be
communicated through daily living.*
—Susan Burgess, therapist, Seattle, Washington

If you have made it to this chapter and have used the book in the
way it was designed, then you have had some interesting talks
with your child. Whether you had one five-minute talk or nine
hour-long talks, you have shared with your child that you understand violence to be a part of life, but that you can also help her to
be as safe as possible. And you've given your child an opportunity
to share her perspectives on life, relationships, and how she deals
with everyday problems.

By this point, you should have a pretty good idea how safe from
violence your child feels. Beneath all the joking, sarcasm, eye
rolling, and reluctance that you may have encountered during your
talks, your child has given you valuable information about how she
wants to be treated by others and how she feels she should treat
others. This tells you who your child is as a person—essentially
what kind of character she has.

When you look in the dictionary you will find interesting definitions for the word *character*. One is "personality" and the other is
"moral strength." As you have talked with your child about the variety of human interaction illustrated in *Ten Talks*, what kinds of
personality traits has your child exhibited? Curiosity? Empathy?
Tolerance? Detachment? Anger? Fear? In each chapter, your child
was asked to make decisions about the behaviors of students and
adults. Often there were ethical and moral decisions to make.

What kinds of morals did your child exhibit? Is your child's moral fiber as strong as you would like?

Preparing for the Talk

As we stated in the beginning of this book, the purpose of *Ten Talks* is to serve as a catalyst for parent-child communication. The goal has been to help you have conversations with your child that empower him, not only giving him the opportunity to talk about important issues, but also reinforcing him as he thinks critically and solves problems. This chapter focuses on your family's beliefs. It gives you an opportunity to review potential problem areas your child may have, and revisit any topic or situation that you feel needs more emphasis.

In this talk you will let your child know that

- he can depend on you to talk about your values.
- you have expectations about her behavior.
- there are family rules—and consequences if he breaks them.

What You Can Expect from This Talk

After the talk your child will

- be able to state your rules about treating others fairly and respectfully.
- know that while different families have different beliefs, your beliefs are the ones that set the standard for right and wrong in your family.

- understand how your beliefs relate to your family rules about violence.

The Importance of Your Beliefs and Values

Your child was born with certain natural instincts, but how those instincts are molded into patterns of behavior is basically up to you. Teachers, coaches, and religious leaders can play an important role, but the parent is the person who is the keeper of the family's core beliefs and values, the building blocks of a child's character. *Ten Talks* respects the values of each parent. This book has been designed to help you communicate your very unique family values about relationships and how people are to be treated.

All the stories in *Ten Talks*, regardless of the issue or situation, presented your child with ethical decisions to make. Your child's responses told you something about his character and—most important—how you can nurture and support your child. The good news is that you can have an impact on his beliefs and values in ways that even TV, the Internet, and his friends and neighbors can't.

Influence of the Media

When was the last time you saw a TV show or film that clearly communicated your beliefs about how people should be treated? Have you found a TV show that supports your view of a loving family and a caring community? With hundreds of TV stations and thousands of videos available, there is a small percentage of programming that offers role models for healthy relationships, or for communicative families, with strong values of respect and non-violence. An important question to ask your child is what kind of characteristics his TV heroes have. What does your child like about favorite TV personalities? If she had to describe her favorite TV show, how would she describe the characters' ethics? How do the traits you admire compare to the traits your child has indentified in her TV heroes?

> *We don't have a TV anymore. I got so fed up with the garbage that was being sent into my living room and my children's minds that I just removed the set. And even though my kids tell me that their friends can't believe that we can live without one, we now spend more evenings and weekends talking, reading, and actually relating to one another as a family.*—Allen, father of two, Fairfax, Virginia

Building a Strong System of Beliefs

Our beliefs and character are what make each of us unique. A person's beliefs and how he supports them are all he has to guide him through life. We all are faced with ethical decisions every day—choices that test our beliefs. Some decisions are small. Do you run red lights when no one is around, tell cashiers when they give you too much change, or tell "white lies" to friends? Your child has noticed.

And while these are small tests, some decisions are big. Do you report suspected child abuse? Do you remain silent about a relative's drinking or spousal abuse? Our character determines how we handle life's complexities. *Ten Talks* stresses talking to your child about beliefs because they're the tools she'll use later to build healthy relationships and live a productive life.

Different Families: Different Values

Your child is presented with many values about violence. You have your own values and rules. But your child's friends, teachers, or the nightly news reporter may have different guidelines. The following scenarios illustrate how a person's beliefs are tested as she receives different messages about violence, death, and killing. The scenarios are somewhat complex and designed to prepare you for questions from your children. Even though these topics might seem very adult, they are issues that have been brought up by elementary, middle, and high school children across the country. Feel free to choose the topics that seem most appropriate for your child.

You're having dinner with your child when she asks you where the hamburgers came from. "From cows," you say. "So you kill them?" your child asks. "What's the difference between that and murder?" she says.

Most parents would say that it's okay to kill animals for food. Others are vegetarians and think it's wrong to eat meat. This conversation can become complicated and raise serious ethical issues about the use of animals for food, clothing, and research.

■

You and your child are watching a TV program about an eleven-year-old who stole a gun and was shooting at animals on a hill. He turned around and saw another child coming toward him. He shot the child, who later died of the wound. The TV announcer asks, "Should he be tried as an adult or be put away and released when he is eighteen?" Your child turns and asks you what you think.

Some parents want to see all murderers, regardless of age, treated the same way. Others feel that minors should be handled with more leniency.

◼

You hear news reports that troops are being sent to join a war in another country. Bombs are being dropped and civilians are being killed. Your child asks you what you think about war and killing. How would you respond?

Some parents see any action the military takes to be for the good of their country. Other parents question why wars are being fought, but say that sometimes innocent civilians might die in a military campaign aimed at establishing peace. Others would rather see diplomatic or economic actions taken because they think these strategies are much more effective in the long run and don't cost human life.

◼

You are reading the newspaper and your child sees a big article about a convicted murderer who is about to be executed. Your child asks what you think about killing convicted prisoners. How would you respond?

Some parents feel that capital punishment is the right of the state and a deterrent to crime. Others feel uncomfortable with killing for any reason. Yet others feel ambivalent or take it case by case.

◼

A visiting grandparent says that one of her older friends is critically ill and in tremendous pain with no hope of recovery. The friend has asked about doctor-assisted suicide. Your child asks if doctor-assisted suicide is the same as murder. How would you respond?

Some parents feel that a person facing certain death after a painful illness has the right to end her own life. Others feel that no one should help someone, even someone in great pain, take his own life. Still others feel that no one should commit suicide under any circumstances.

All of these issues are very sensitive and complex. It may be years before your child really understands how she feels about them. In fact, values clarification takes a lifetime. It's important that you work to clarify your own values because as your children start building the foundation of their own beliefs, they'll be looking to you for guidance.

Last-minute Checkups before the Talk

Before you start the talk, think about your own upbringing and how issues of character, morals, and family beliefs were presented to you.

- Did your parents tell you that you should treat people in a certain way?
- Did they have strong beliefs about right and wrong, and communicate those beliefs to you?
- Did they pass on a set of family beliefs—religious or not—to help guide you and help you make ethical decisions?

How are you communicating your family beliefs to your child?

- Do you talk to your child about the difference between right and wrong?

- Are you raising your child with a set of family beliefs—religious or not—to help him make ethical decisions?
- Do you think your behaviors make it clear how your child is to treat people?

This is a good time to think about your childhood experiences with learning about morals, beliefs, and character. Do you have any stories that you could share with your child? For example:

- A story about an adult who talked about morals and ethics with you
- An experience talking about values with a parent
- A time when an adult explained the difference between right and wrong
- A story about how you developed your values and beliefs

Keep these stories in mind as you talk with your child.

What Are Your Family Rules?

In previous chapters we have offered sample family rules shared by parents from around the country. This chapter will not offer family rules on developing character. Instead, take a few minutes to think about your own unique set of beliefs, values, and morals and the kind of character you want your child to have.

In the stories in this talk, a parent and child have a meaningful conversation about family beliefs and values. The stories are open-ended, allowing you to bring up any issues important to you.

As you think about the moral direction you are giving your child, consider what kinds of family rules need to be in place to offer your child the guidelines she needs. For example, how do the family rules about preventing violence complement the other family rules you have? Do you feel that you have the rules you need in place, and the ability to enforce them? If you need help of any kind, where can you go to find it? Parents of a defiant child, especially a young person with a predisposition toward violent behavior, may very well need help communicating and enforcing family rules.

Clearly, introducing family rules to a compliant six-year-old is going to be a lot easier than to an aggressive adolescent. But as many parents have found, you can change your parenting style at any time, whether that means having regular family talks or developing new family rules. This may sound a little formal, but you may want to consider writing your official family rules down on a piece of paper. It's a visual aid you can use when reviewing the rules with your child. You might also create a draft and ask for your child's feedback on both the rules and the consequences for breaking them. With their input, you can create the final set of rules.

If it were possible for a book to take a break for a public service announcement, this would be the spot in *Ten Talks* where we would say, "Please put down the book, pull out a piece of paper and pencil, and jot down your family rules on violence and safety."

We didn't have family rules except for taking out the garbage and making the beds. It's been a good experience to actually sit down with our kids and lay out some new guidelines.
—Sam, father of two, Kansas City, Missouri

Every so often I realize the kids are older and need a different set of rules. I print them out and post them on the refrigerator. We were hav-

*ing problems with my children's friends breaking our house rules, so
now I point out the rules so there is no misunderstanding.*
—Pam, mother of two, Gaithersburg, Maryland

The Talk

A hearty congratulations for making it to talk number ten. After
nine chapters and talks you have had the opportunity to hear how
your child responds to a variety of situations and problems, and how
he makes moral choices. This talk will give you a chance to reinforce
any areas you think may need special attention. If you thought your
child didn't quite get the importance of following certain Internet
rules, then you can address cyberspace safety. If you thought that
your child struggled with when to be an observer and when to be
heroic, then you can revisit some of Chapter Two's concepts for a re-
fresher course. If you feel that your daughter wasn't confident setting
personal boundaries, especially around aggressive males, then revis-
iting the stories about the baby-sitter in Chapter Six might be helpful. Think about any trouble spots encountered during any of the
previous talks, and use this time to address them.

Introduce the Talk

Find a time for an uninterrupted ten minutes or so. With this book
in hand, tell your child, "Good news! I need you for about five or
ten minutes to walk through the last official *Ten Talks* conversation." You may get a variety of reactions, from "Yeah, right!" to
"You promise?" It should be noted that some parents have re-

ported that these talks are a highlight of their child's day. For some parents busy with work, parenting, and other activities, the talk becomes a great opportunity to shower their kids with attention, something younger children usually enjoy.

Next, you could say, "I've got something I want to discuss. Have you ever heard the term *beliefs*?"

Be prepared to hear "No" or "What's that?" This might be a sophisticated term for an elementary school child. You could offer, "What do the words *beliefs* and *values* mean?" Your child may offer some examples. If so, proceed with the next section.

If he doesn't offer any examples of the term *beliefs,* you can offer up something like this:

"Beliefs are what makes a person feel and act the way he does. How you act on your beliefs is what makes up your personality. Your beliefs are like your moral compass. Your beliefs help you tell right from wrong—without a written rulebook. Have you heard the phrase 'She has very strong beliefs'? Your beliefs are part of your character, your unique personality. Words like *beliefs, values,* and *character* are all tools to help us understand who we are, how we feel about things, and how we should behave toward others."

Review These Words

Please review the terms in this section. Discussing all the terms with your child is optional. You know what's appropriate for your child's age and maturity level. More than likely, even the youngest children have heard these words on TV.

beliefs: acceptance that certain things are true and real
character: personality, moral strength

ethics: moral standards, system of morals
morals: what's right or wrong
principles: a person's basic truths, or rules of conduct

Why Is Talking about Family Beliefs Important?

For some children, talking about family beliefs seems as relevant as talking about what kind of health care system they have in Sweden. Your child may ask, "Why do we have to talk about this stuff?" Some responses might be:

- Beliefs are what you hold to be true. And I want to know if we share the same ones.
- People's beliefs help them sort through problems. I want to know how you are doing.
- I want to know what kinds of beliefs you admire.
- Talking about beliefs helps families set standards for behavior.
- Talking about beliefs helps children and parents clarify right and wrong.

The Stories

In the next part of the talk, you'll be reading short stories to your child and discussing them together. You don't have to read all of the stories. Pick the ones that you think are appropriate for your child. The stories are very simple. Feel free to embellish them, adding details that you think might make the story more believable to your child.

The following stories present the same situation: a parent and child talking. They illustrate a mother talking with a daughter, a mother talking with a son, a father talking with a daughter, and a father talking with a son. These stories are a little different from the stories in the previous nine chapters in that the parent can take a very active role in choosing the topic to be explored. Choose the story and set-up that make you most comfortable. You may wish to review the sample talks at the end of the chapter to see what areas were explored by other parents.

The following four scenarios are identical except for the genders of the characters. You may wish to focus on only one scenario—say, the one that most closely mirrors your situation. (For example, if you are a mom talking with a daughter, you only may be interested in doing the "Mom and Daughter Talk." A father may wish to use the "Dad and Son Talk.") You might find it interesting to use the other three stories to explore and discuss with your child attitudes of males and females. We have heard from many single moms that their sons and daughters are very curious about how men think and feel. If the father is not available for talks, consider enlisting an adult male (grandfather, uncle, older cousin, or trusted friend) to talk with your child about family beliefs. Single dads could enlist the help of a grandmother, aunt, older cousin, or trusted friend.

The Story about a Mom and Daughter Talking

This talk gives you an opportunity to address any concerns that may not have been addressed in *Ten Talks*, or to review any areas you feel need reinforcing.

"A mother is reading *Ten Talks*." (You can decide what chapter she is reading, "Family Beliefs," "Roles," "Media," or whatever topic you wish to review with your child.) "The book covers many issues that focus on how people should treat one another. Her daughter comes in and sits down at the table."

The discussion questions that follow will allow you to explore any areas you think are important. You may choose to direct the talk by telling your child what you think the parent is thinking. For example, if you are worried about your daughter's ability to set personal boundaries, you can say, "The mom in this story is thinking, 'I'm worried about my daughter.'" At that point, you might let your child direct the activity, by telling you what the parent and child are thinking and saying.

Ask these questions of your child:

- What does the parent say?
- What does the child say?
- What is the parent thinking?
- What is the child thinking?

Now that your child has completed this scenario, ask the following questions:

- Does the parent have any special concerns?
- Does the child have any special concerns?
- Does the child understand why a book about how people should treat one another would be important to talk about?
- How does the child know the difference between right and wrong?

- How often does this type of talk really happen?
- Have you ever seen or been in a situation like this? If so, what did you talk about? How did you feel after the talk?

The Story about a Mom and Son Talking

This talk gives you an opportunity to address any concerns that may not have been addressed in *Ten Talks*, or to review any areas you feel need reinforcing.

"A mother is reading *Ten Talks*." (You can decide what chapter she is reading.) "The book covers many issues that focus on how people should treat one another. Her son comes in and sits down at the table."

The discussion questions that follow will allow you to explore any areas you think are important. You may choose to direct the talk by telling your child what you think the parent is thinking. For example, if you are worried about your son's ability to follow safety rules on the Internet, you can say, "The mom in this story is thinking, 'I'm worried about my son and his computer.'" At that point, you might let your child direct the activity, by telling you what the parent and child are thinking and saying.

Ask these questions of your child:

- What does the parent say?

- What does the child say?
- What is the parent thinking?
- What is the child thinking?

Now that your child has completed this scenario, ask the following questions:

- Does the parent have any special concerns?
- Does the child have any special concerns?
- Does the child understand why a book about "how people should treat one another" would be important to talk about?
- How does the child know the difference between right and wrong?
- How often does this type of talk really happen?
- Have you ever seen or been in a situation like this? If so, what did you talk about?

The Story about a Dad and Daughter Talking

This talk gives you an opportunity to address any concerns that may not have been addressed in *Ten Talks*, or to review any areas you feel need reinforcing.

"A dad is reading *Ten Talks*." (You can decide what chapter he is reading.) "The book covers many issues that focus on how people should treat one another." His daughter comes in and sits down at the table."

The discussion questions that follow will allow you to explore any areas you think are important. You may choose to direct the talk by telling your child what you think the parent is thinking. For example, if you are worried about your daughter's ability to set personal boundaries, you can say, "The dad in this story is thinking, 'I'm worried about my daughter getting into situations that might be dangerous.'" At that point, you might let your child direct the activity, by telling you what the parent and child are thinking and saying.

Ask these questions of your child:

- What does the parent say?
- What does the child say?
- What is the parent thinking?
- What is the child thinking?

Now that your child has completed this scenario, ask the following questions:

- Does the parent have any special concerns?
- Does the child have any special concerns?
- Does the child understand why a book about how people should treat one another would be important to talk about?
- How does the child know the difference between right and wrong?
- How often does this type of talk really happen?
- Have you ever seen or been in a situation like this? If so, what did you talk about?

The Story about a Dad and Son Talking

This talk gives you an opportunity to address any concerns that may not have been addressed in *Ten Talks*, or to review any areas you feel need reinforcing.

"A dad is reading *Ten Talks*." (You can decide what chapter he is reading.) "The book covers many issues that focus on how people should treat one another. His son comes in and sits down at the table."

The discussion questions that follow will allow you to explore any areas you think are important. You may choose to direct the talk by telling your child what you think the parent is thinking. For example, if you are worried about your son's ability to respect other people's personal boundaries, you can say, "The dad in this story is thinking, 'I'm worried about my son getting into trouble.'" At that point, you might let your child direct the activity by telling you what the parent and child are thinking and saying.

Ask these questions of your child:

- What does the parent say?
- What does the child say?
- What is the parent thinking?
- What is the child thinking?

Now that your child has completed this scenario, ask the following questions:

- Does the parent have any special concerns?
- Does the child have any special concerns?
- Does the child understand why a book about how people should treat one another would be important to talk about?
- How does the child know the difference between right and wrong?
- How often does this type of talk really happen?
- Have you ever seen or been in a situation like this? If so, what did you talk about?

Clarify Your Family's Values

Discuss these questions with your child as a way of sharing your values. We have included a number of potential responses from children to help you formulate your own responses.

Ask your child: "What happens when a child is raised without any guidance on how to behave, how to tell right from wrong, or how to treat others with respect?"

Child response #1: I don't know.
Parent: It depends. For some children, having no direction from a caring parent can be very harmful. The child never learns right from wrong. In other families, a child may learn to parent himself. This is very difficult and usually requires the support of teachers, social workers, therapists, or other trusted adults. But a child can create a strong compassionate character against the odds.

Child response #2: He goes crazy and hurts people.
Parent: That can happen. Without a loving parent to raise a

child, a person can become emotionally disturbed. It's a struggle to parent yourself—though some people do it and develop into healthy adults. We all need love and caring to grow up feeling secure. Not everyone who grows up in a violent family becomes violent, but people who are violent tend to have grown up in violent situations.

The Bare Minimum: A Quick Quiz for Kids
Ask your child the following questions to assess her knowledge of her own beliefs.

1. What are some beliefs that show a person is respectful and caring?
   Sample answers:
- I believe in treating people with respect
- I believe a person should always be honest

2. How does someone learn to be respectful of others?
   Sample answers:
- By watching their parents, teachers, or other adults
- By spending time with adults and children who show respect and compassion

Talk about Your Family Rules

As you know, *Ten Talks* is filled with sample family rules in every chapter. Take some time to think about what family rules you need to invent, introduce, reintroduce, change, omit, add, or emphasize. You also may want to review the consequences of breaking the rules and go over all of this with your child.

After the Talk

A Moment to Reflect

Take a moment to reflect on the talk you just had with your child. How do you feel about it?

- What surprised you about your child's values and beliefs? Does her sense of right and wrong make you comfortable?
- How do you think your child felt about the talk?
- How much of the time were you listening to your child?
- What follow-up talk would you like to have?

Warning Signs

The talks may also reveal potential problems that your child is facing. In some families there may be what is called a crisis of character. Some children show little empathy for others, which might prove troubling. There may be cause for concern if you hear from the school, or from other parents or child-care providers, that your child

- shows little regard for the lives of animals.
- feels entitled to do anything he wants, even at the expense of others.
- is extraordinarily passive and submissive to others.
- is obsessed with beliefs that show disrespect for human life.

Always use your instincts as a parent when it comes to looking for warning signs of serious trouble. In any of these situations, you need to find out what is happening by talking with your child. If after your discussion you feel your child needs more help than you alone can offer, visit the school counselor or look further into one of the many resources available in your community.

Finding Help

If needed, support and help for your child is available. Most teachers, school counselors, and principals, religious leaders, mental health, social workers, and juvenile justice workers can refer parents to caring professionals with expertise in working with young people.

Success Stories

You have made it through *Ten Talks*. Excellent work! You now have greater insight into how your child views the world and is navigating through it. You have opened up communication about violence—which means you can now talk about pretty much anything. If we have sparked your interest in studies about child development or parent-child communication, we encourage you to visit your local bookstore or library, where you will find a wealth of information on these topics.

Around the country, we are hearing that the *Ten Talks* approach can serve as a catalyst for productive family talks, helping parents and their children build stronger relationships and opening up the lines of communication. More and more schools, religious organizations, community groups, and workplaces are sponsoring workshops for parents to help them strengthen family communication. As a parent, you have the most important job on earth. The work you are doing with your child affects everyone. Always remember that you are supported by other parents—we're all in this together. *Ten Talks* salutes your hard work and wishes you the best for your ongoing talks with your child. Know that your work helps strengthen not only your family but the entire community as well.

A Final Note

From a young age, my children let me know what they thought about the things happening around them at school. We talked about violence, and what we can do to be safe and to make our communities safer places. It's going to take young people and adults working in partnership to make a real difference. The best way to start is for parents and children to really listen to each other.
—Patty Murray, U.S. senator and mother of two

Violence is a very complex topic. Certainly there are no easy answers when it comes to keeping every child safe from violence and preventing our young children from growing into violent teens and adults. But we know some things that can be done to make your child's world a safer place. Change happens on many levels. *Ten Talks* has focused on the change you would like to nurture in the family. This is something you're already part of if you are holding this book. Change also happens at the school level, the neighborhood level, and at the city, state, and national levels as well.

No matter where you sit, you are part of the solution. Future editions of *Ten Talks* will share additional strategies that are succeeding in making neighborhoods safer places for children. You are encouraged to become involved in your community in ways that suit your skills and interests. Your compassion and energy are needed because there is a lot of work to be done. All of the team members involved in the making of *Ten Talks* would like to end this book with a wish that you and your family enjoy good health—and great conversations! Good luck with the most important work in the world: being a parent.

We would enjoy hearing how your ten talks are going. Let us know about your successes, challenges, and creative approaches by visiting www.tentalks.com

Sample Talks

Between Parents and Children

If you are wondering how a talk based on this chapter might really sound, take a look at the following excerpts from real family talks.

Discussing the Story about a Mom and Daughter Talking

Participants: a mother and her fourth-grade daughter.

Mom: I'm going to read you a story. This one is about a mom. She's reading a book. And the book is about how people should treat each other. And her daughter comes in and sits down at the table. What do you think this mother might say to her daughter as she comes in?

Child: I think she would say, "Okay, here, I'm reading a book about how you treat each other."

Mom: What do you think the child's going to say to her when she says that?

Child: She says, "Uh-oh."

Mom: Why would she say it like that?

Child: Because she probably thinks it is a boring book.

Mom: Do you think a child would understand what a book about how to treat others is about?

Child: Well it depends. In my school we have this "Character Counts" thing and it's how to treat each other.

Mom: Yeah.

Child: And our counselor, Mrs. F., does all these drug-free things and she even has mediators who come out on the playground and help kids with their problems, fighting, and stuff.

Mom: How does the child know the difference between right and wrong? How do they know that? Do they think they just know that or are they taught it? What do you think?

Child: The same thing that I just said. Well, some people may know it because they have that method in their school about "Character Counts" and they know the difference between right and wrong.

Mom: But before you even get to school, before you went to any school, did you know what was right and wrong?

Child: Yes, you told me about it.

Mom: So is that how children learn—from their parents?

Child: Yes.

Mom: Can children sometimes learn by watching other children?

Child: No.

Mom: Why not?

Child: Because some kids do things wrong and, if the child is young and they haven't been taught any of this, then they might think that is right.

Mom: That's a good point. You need somebody to say, that kind of behavior is good behavior and that kind of behavior is bad behavior, don't you? Especially when you're very young, before you've gone to school. How often do you think parents really talk to their kids, saying, "That's good" and "That's not so good" and "We really need to remember that."

Child: Well, some parents do talk a lot about this with their kids.

Mom: Why might some kids' parents not talk about the difference between right and wrong with the kids?

Child: 'Cause they may not be raised by a family that cared about it, so they were never really taught it.

Lessons Learned from This Sample Talk

This talk represents an important first step in which a parent approaches the topic of talking with her child about character issues, and ethical issues about right and wrong. Further talks can explore how she might get along with kids and adults whose ideas of right and wrong are different from hers and her families.

Discussing the Story about a Mom and Son Talking

Participants: a mother and her fifth-grade son.

Mom: A mother is reading a book about how people should treat one another. Her son comes in and sits down at the table. What does the parent say? What is the parent thinking?

Child: (in a silly, sing-song way) Do you want to listen to a story?

Mom: Oh, okay. What is the son thinking?

Child: It depends. Is he a good boy or bad boy?

Mom: He's a good boy, but once in a while he has a few problems.

Mom: How is the son feeling? (long pause) Do you think he feels good about the kind of person he is?

Child: Oh, so-so.

Mom: I'm going to stick a little something in here. The parent is a little concerned about how many violent video games the son is playing. So when the parent is reading this book she's wondering if all these wrestling and killing-focused video games are affecting her son. So how is the parent feeling now that she's talking to her son?

Child: I don't know.

Mom: Does the son have any special concerns now, about this conversation?

Child: He's thinking, "Oh, no." And he's saying, "Oh. Okay."

Mom: Well, do you think he's concerned that his mom won't let him watch and play as many games?

Child: Yes. (They both laugh.)

Mom: Does the son understand what a book about how people should treat others could be about?

Child: Yes.

Mom: And how might renting video games that have a lot of violence have anything to do with how people treat others?

Child: Not much.

Mom: You don't think so?

Child: I don't know.

Mom: How does the son know the difference between right and wrong?

Child: Well, if he feels he did something right, then it's right according to him unless it's wrong. And if he feels it's wrong, then he won't do it.

Mom: How often do mothers and their sons have this kind of talk about how to treat others? (long pause) Why are you staring at me? (Both laugh.)

Child: Not often.

Mom: But do you understand how watching a video game where people go around killing each other might be a reflection on the values that parent has?

Child: I don't know.

Mom: Is this enough of this conversation? You are nodding your head so I guess so. We can talk about this another time. Thanks.

Lessons Learned from This Sample Talk

In this talk the mother began with general questions about how to treat others and moved to the topic of violent video games, an area of concern to her. This talk was very productive in that it brought up many issues and values the son holds. Further talks could explore the parents' criteria for understanding the difference between right and wrong, and why video games that simulate killing people could affect her son's sensitivity to violence. The mother and son enjoyed some laughs during the talk and the mother knew when to end the talk.

Discussing the Story about a Dad and Daughter Talking

Participants: a father and his sixth-grade and third-grade daughters.

Dad: A father is reading a book about how people should treat one another. His daughter comes in and sits down at the table. Now, what does the parent say?

Younger daughter: "Come sit down with me and listen so you'll know how to treat one another."

Dad: And what does the daughter say?

Younger daughter: If it were me, I'd say, "I don't want to."

Older daughter: If it were me, I'd say, "Maybe later, I'm going to go wash the dishes."

Dad: Okay. So what do you think the parent is thinking?

Younger daughter: He thinks, "I'm going to teach my child how to treat people."

Dad: And what do you think the child is thinking?

Younger daughter: "I don't want to talk because I want to go do something else."

Dad: Does the father have any special concerns?

Younger daughter: Follow all the Golden Rules.

Dad: Does the child have any concerns?

Older daughter: Not really.

Dad: Do you think the child understands what a book about how to treat people would be about?

Younger daughter: Not really.

Dad: Would you understand about a book about character?

Older daughter: Yeah.

Dad: Why?

Older daughter: Because we already learned about this stuff in school.

Dad: So how does a child know the difference between right and wrong?

Older daughter: Being taught by the parents.

Dad: And how often do you think that would happen?

Older daughter: Not very often. Like, some parents don't put in the time to stay with their children and teach them. People just go to work and say school will teach them everything.

Lessons Learned from This Sample Talk

In this talk, the daughters mentioned that some parents are too busy for their kids. It might be interesting in further talks to see if these daughters feel that their parents are too busy for them. The older daughter mentioned that she already learned "this stuff" (about character and how to treat people) in school. Asking what "this stuff" includes, and asking the younger daughter what she has learned about character, can also be discussed in future talks.

Discussing the Story about a Dad and Son Talking

Participants: a father and his fourth-grade son.

Dad: This is a story about how we should treat one another. The dad is reading a book about how we all should care for other people. It says that people should be nice to each other and get along and do for other people as you would want done for yourself. The son comes in and asks what the dad is reading. What is that dad in this story saying?

Child: Well, um. I don't know.

Dad: The dad says, "I'm reading a book about how to treat people." He asks his son what the son knows about treating people with respect.

Child: I understand, because at my school I'm a mediator and I'm part of SGA (Student Government Association) so I know about respect.

Dad: Do you know the difference between right and wrong?

Child: Yeah. When we were like fighting and calling names, that's wrong. When you're caring and nice, that's right.

Dad: And you know when you're wrong? You can tell when you're wrong when you do something, when you act some way, when you say something. You know when it's wrong. What if you saw someone else doing wrong? How would that make you feel?

Child: If it was to somebody else I would just try and make him stop doing it.

Dad: Tell him not to be mean to other people.

Child: Yeah.

Dad: Yes, and you know how to act and what to do because we have talked about it, right?

Child: Yeah.

Lessons Learned from This Sample Talk

This talk started with the story about a dad reading a book about treating people with respect. The parent was able to find out about his son's involvement in the school government, his sense of justice, and his understanding of "respect." The son had some good examples of "right" and "wrong" which can be further explored in later discussions. This talk was an excellent starting point and set the stage for future talks about character traits valued by the father, as well as beliefs, morals and ethics—all important concepts for a parent and child to explore together. Taking stock periodically is important to make sure the child is firm in his beliefs.